Marketing and Communications

The Right Social Media Content at the Right Time

Social Media Strategy Certification
Your Story. Your Certification.
Exam Voucher www.nismonline.org/shop

National Institute for Social Media

Books in this series:

- The Rules of Social Media Compliance & Governance: Know What You Need to Know
- Social Media Project Management: Establish and Maintain Successful Projects and Campaigns
- Marketing & Communications: The Right Social Media Content at the Right Time
- Strategic Planning: Social Media Success with SMART Goals, KPIs and Data Analysis
- Social Media Research & Analysis: Make Powerful Decisions by Listening to Consumer and Competitor Behavior
- Online Community Management: Grow and Develop an Active Audience on Social Media

Marketing and Communications

The Right Social Media Content at the Right Time

Dr. Amy Jauman

NISM
National Institute for Social Media

ISBN: 978-1-946649-08-9

Special thanks to the following content reviewers from the National Institute for Social Media community. We appreciate your feedback and continued support!

- Jennifer Radke, SMS
- Kimberly Behzadi, MBA, SMS
- Forrest Flinn, SMS, PHR/SHRM-CP
- Kaley Halliburton

What is the National Institute for Social Media (NISM)?

The National Institute for Social Media (NISM) is an organization dedicated to social media certification and education for professional social media practitioners. In partnership with organizations and lifelong learning enthusiasts, they've created a community for professional development and set the standards for social media education, assessment and certification, and consulting. NISM provides the foremost Social Media Strategy (SMS) certification exam in the US, which allows social media professionals to obtain a recognized professional standard in this continually developing field.

Why does NISM provide a certification for social media professionals?

A certification in any industry is an unbiased, standard measurement of an individual's ability to perform specific skills. NISM realized the need for a certification within the realm of social media as more and more individuals entered the field with varying levels of experience. How could experienced social media professionals demonstrate their knowledge? How could hiring managers identify individuals with the skill set they desired in social media strategy? A professional certification is the perfect solution. The SMS certification covers six content domains (Compliance and Governance, Community Management, Marketing and Communication, Research and Analysis,

Project Management, and Strategic Planning) that ensure each person who successfully passes the exam has the depth and breadth needed to be considered a professional social media strategist. In addition to passing this rigorous exam, individuals must continue to update and enhance their skills in order to stay current with their certification, through continuing education courses, workshops, and conferences. The National Institute for Social Media also requires all NISM-certified Social Media Strategists (SMS) to adhere to a strict code of ethics.

NISM has built its community of social media professionals around five core values:

Trust – for both the confidence in the works we do for our customers and the value we add to the industry as a whole through hard work, honesty, and integrity.

Community – it is our belief that in order to create a positive community we need to not only find ways to use our skills to support each other, but to also encourage others around us to participate and get involved as well.

Respect – as a fundamental building block for all relationships, it is imperative that we treat others as we want to be treated and to acknowledge and promote the great work of our colleagues and peers.

Quality – at our core we recognize that the value we provide to our community hinges on quality. Our dedication to standards and external industry credentialing is key to our success.

Lifelong Learning – with the rate at which social media changes, we realize that if we are not in constant learning mode we will fall behind and fail to stay relevant.

We promote lifelong learning within our community and as an industry at large.

Who's the author?

Dr. Amy Jauman is a certified Social Media Strategist and lead instructor at the National Institute for Social Media. She is a social media consultant, writer and professor and her formal education includes a master's degree in experiential education, so you'll find plenty of real-world application prompts. She also has a doctorate in organization development, so there's a lot of information about how to work with people in a variety of business environments. Her interest in helping people prepare for and pass the SMS certification exam was piqued in 2011 when she began looking for ways she could establish her credibility in social media.

Dr. Jauman discovered that many of her peers working in social media and students venturing out as marketing professionals had the same need for social media credentials that accurately represented their knowledge and experience. When presented with the chance to write these books and provide students and professionals with a practical guide to the six content domains covered in the SMS certification exam, she jumped at the opportunity.

Who should read this book?

There are likely three groups of people who would benefit most from reading this book, although it is of value to anyone with an interest in marketing and communications using social media platforms.

Anyone prepping to take the SMS certification exam. If you're thinking about taking the SMS exam, you've probably discovered that marketing and communications is one of six content domains covered in the exam. Whatever your level of experience in marketing and communications, this book can be a great way to quickly and easily check out what's covered on the exam. It can also help you identify areas you might want to learn more about before your exam.

Anyone considering a role that is entirely or in part associated with marketing and communications. It's possible that the depth and breadth of the SMS certification exam doesn't interest you. If you're more interested in one area of social media – working exclusively in marketing and communications as opposed to the broader role of being a certified social media strategist – this book can provide you with insights specific to your area of interest. One of the reasons we transitioned from a single, large textbook to six smaller books was to connect with the social media professionals interested in joining our community through their expertise in one or two of the content domains.

Anyone considering hiring a marketing and communications expert. It's possible that you aren't even interested in social media strategy or certification – but you're smart enough to know it's important. This book can act as a great guide for any leader in any industry considering adding a social media marketing and communications expert to the team.

However you're connected to the National Institute for Social Media (NISM) and whatever you'd like to learn from this book, we invite you to connect with us. Find us on Facebook at facebook.com/NISMPulse, Twitter @NISMPulse or any of the sites listed at nismonline.org.

The National Institute for Social Media Code of Ethics

The Code of Ethics is intended to reflect the standards and behavior that National Institute for Social Media ("NISM") certified practitioners and program applicants expect of each other as they perform their duties and that reaffirm the value of holding an NISM credential. The purpose of the Code of Ethics is to ensure public confidence in the integrity and service of NISM-certified professionals while performing their duties.

The Code of Ethics identifies the types of circumstances that may compromise the reliability of NISM's ability to establish, or certify, a certificate holder's or program applicant's ability to perform the essential tasks of the vocation with at least minimal competency. For purposes of this Code of Ethics, "essential tasks" are defined as the general vocational duties that are expected to be performed by NISM-certified professionals. "Minimal competency" is defined as the ability to perform the essential tasks effectively, with minimal supervision.

NISM does not monitor on-the-job behavior or actions. Adherence to these ethical standards is expected from all certificate holders and applicants. Any violation may be subject to removal of his or her certified status.

All NISM certificate holders and applicants are expected to adhere to the following standards of professional conduct and ethics:

1. We represent ourselves truthfully, honestly, and to the best of our abilities throughout the entire certification process, and in performance of the essential tasks described in section 3 of the Candidate handbook.

2. We adhere to all exam site rules, making no attempt to complete an exam dishonestly or to assist any other person in doing so.
3. We protect proprietary or confidential information that has been entrusted to us as if it were our own.
4. We state only what we know to be true, and are clear about opinions and assumptions vs. facts.
5. We are transparent about who we are, and whom or what we represent online.
6. We take ownership of our online activities, the content we have created, and any missteps we have made along the way.
7. We uphold the policies, rules, regulations and laws that govern our activities.
8. We report unethical or illegal conduct to appropriate authorities.

Contents

Introduction

Marketing and Communications

When you look at the content domains covered on the certified SMS exam, the majority seem pretty straightforward: Strategic Planning, Community Management, Compliance and Governance, Project Management, and Research and Analysis. But the domain of Marketing and Communications gives some people pause. After all, isn't marketing and communications covered by the entire exam? How does it vary from community management? Is this just one big book of tips?

These are all great questions – and just to make sure we're all on the same page, we'll cover them one at a time.

Isn't the entire SMS exam about marketing and communications?

The National Institute for Social Media (NISM) works hard to support professionals working in social media. A large part of the support provided is educating people from a variety of backgrounds about the importance of maintaining a social media *strategy*, not just an active presence online. The exam covers the six content domains that allow professionals to create and manage a successful strategy. Within Marketing and Communications, a strategist learns how to

- Prepare your marketplace and your team before a product launch
- Gauge audience interest – and adjust accordingly

- Create the best content
- Share your content in the best way

How is that different from community management?

The NISM Candidate Handbook describes community management in part as *"the process of ensuring that the two-way online communication between the organization and its customers/stakeholders always flows smoothly. The manager serves as a professional representative for the organization's products or services, while simultaneously gathering feedback for further development of products or services for evaluation."*

For a community manager to be successful, they must have a solid marketing and communications base to start. The focus of community management is on two-way communication, whereas marketing and communications includes priming the marketplace, gauging audience interest, sharing stories, and preparing for campaigns. The two areas are undeniably intertwined but very different.

Is this just one big book of tips?

All of the NISM books are very practical, but this one probably has more tips than the others. However, it's more than a compilation of helpful tips. Remember that the SMS exam focuses on social media *strategy*, not tactics. Of course, a good strategy leads to effective tactics and oftentimes it's hard to separate the two, but the focus of this book is to provide a strategic approach that is appropriate for all social media platforms, even as they continually evolve.

Understanding the strategy behind your work – *why* you're completing various marketing and communications tasks – is important to your success and a critical component assessed on the SMS certification exam. But don't worry – we know that specific techniques are also important and you'll find plenty of suggestions here, too. In fact, reading further in the description of marketing and communications in the NISM Candidate Handbook, you'll see tactical approaches are also covered in the exam.

"Priming the marketplace, gauging audience interest, sharing stories and preparing for campaigns and/or sharing your campaign announcements via internet-driven technology such as blogs, RSS, web video productions, podcasts and social networking platforms are essential to the content of social media marketing.

"Candidates will be measured on their understanding of essential tasks within this competency domain. The marketing and communication domain consists of identifying who is in your core audience, segmenting your core audience, identifying what social media content your audience perceives as valuable, and determining the methods that your core audience prefers to interact with the organization. The process of putting organizational culture into words that can be used as a guide for social media activities, creating branding consistency across all social media platforms, and using traditional media in conjunction with social media are also assessed.

"Candidates will also be tested on the practices of offering social media content that customers perceive as valuable as opposed to selling, providing content that informs, entertains, and helps, and publishing content to the organization's blog(s), microblog(s) and social networking platforms.

"Furthermore, candidates are tested on the methods of ensuring all written and video social media content is brief, concise and accurate, taking out advertisements on social media platforms, and reporting campaign status updates on a regular basis to management and key stakeholders."

As a social media professional, it's important not to get caught in the weeds of tactical work. But in the case of marketing and communications we understand the value of tactical ideas, so you'll find plenty of them!

NISM 2016 Social Media Job Study

54.5% of participants ranked planning and goal setting as a task of high importance. This is an increase of 34.3% from the 2012 study.

25.9% of those surveyed spend more than 10 hours each week on project management tasks.

Each content domain increased in importance from 2012 to 2016.

The most important task within Marketing & Communications was

Branding

66.5% identified it as highly important.

The NISM 2016 Social Media Job Study

43 states.
20 industries.
533 men and women.
Managers, employees and consultants.

68.8% of participants cited acting appropriately without direction as highly important. It was perceived as important in 2012 as well, but only 43.6% chose **highly important.**

Responding to comments increased from low to high importance between 2012 and 2016.

#NISM2016JS

Content domains explored through the job study are the same as the SMS exam.

Project Management
Governance & Compliance
Marketing & Communications
Research & Analysis
Strategic Planning
Community

The value of 2-way communication with customers increased from medium to high importance.

www.nismonline.org

Part One
Preparation

Chapter 1

NISM Job Study Results

In the 2016 NISM Social Media Job Study, designed to understand the key responsibilities of social media strategists, we asked about the prevalence and importance of marketing and communications. Marketing and communications was described to survey participants as follows:

> *"Marketing & communications includes priming the marketplace, gauging audience interest, sharing stories and preparing for campaigns and/or sharing your campaign announcements via internet-driven technology. Blogs, RSS, web video productions, podcasts and social networking platforms are essential to the content of social media marketing."*

The survey questions focused on the following six aspects of marketing and communications:

- Take out advertisements on social media platforms
- Ensure branding consistency across all social media platforms
- Ensure all written and video social media content is brief, concise, and accurate
- Work with key stakeholders to identify who company customers are and report progress
- Publish content to company blog(s), microblogging platforms (e.g., Twitter), and social networking platforms (e.g., Facebook)
- Read, comment, and respond to the content or comments of your industry peers

In the first social media job study conducted by NISM in 2012, marketing and communications was generally ranked as highly important. One important point to mention is that this sub-category was given a higher level of importance compared to the previous survey completed.

- The percentage of people who ranked taking out advertisements on social media platforms as highly important nearly doubled, increasing from 17.1% to 34%.
- 66.5% of survey respondents in 2016 believe that branding consistency across all social media platforms is of high importance. 26.5% indicated it was of high importance in 2012. The change would indicate that the perceived importance of branding has increased significantly.
- In a world now saturated with content, people are becoming harder to engage. It's no surprise that 72% of the survey respondents indicated that ensuring all written and video social media content is brief, concise, and accurate is of high importance – an increase from 31.1% in 2012.
- In 2012, the largest percentage of respondents indicated that working with key stakeholders to identify who company customers are was of medium importance. By 2016, the largest group ranked reporting as highly important.
- In 2012, 37.8% of survey respondents felt that reading, commenting, and responding to the content or comments of your industry peers was of low importance, and only 18.9% thought it was highly important. In 2016, those numbers reversed. 22.2% felt interaction on peer platforms was of low importance while 36.8% felt it was highly important.

Survey participants were given the opportunity to share additional thoughts about the importance of marketing and communications. Some of their additional feedback included comments related to the importance of engaging C-suite employees as advocates and the importance of constantly supporting their digital community.

When we explored the varying value of importance of the marketing and communications domain expressed by our survey participants, some important questions arose:

- Who are the key stakeholders within an organization and what's the best way to help them understand the importance of supporting the organization's social media presence?
- For any size team, what's the most efficient way to create the best content?
- Where should social media professionals share content – and how often?

The previous questions are examples of how social media professionals might explore and further understand marketing and communications within their organization. NISM and particularly the SMS certification exam focus on marketing and communications in general and do not focus on a particular industry or organization, relying on individuals to make the industry-specific adjustments required.

We will address these issues in the following sections of this book, to help you understand how to create effective marketing and communications content. We will explore:

- How to identify your core audience and key stakeholders
- What social media content your customers perceive as valuable
- How to ensure that written and video content is brief, concise, and accurate
- How to identify your core audience's preferred methods of interacting with the company

- How a communications plan can support a team of any size
- Branding consistency across all social media platforms
- Publishing content to company blog(s), microblogging platforms (e.g., Twitter), and social networking platforms (e.g., Facebook)
- Performing real-time monitoring of brand sentiment
- Taking out advertisements on social media platforms
- Using traditional media in conjunction with social media
- Reporting progress on a regular basis to management and key stakeholders

---

Chapter 1 Discussion

1. Review the entire NISM job study. What additional information about marketing and communications or quotes from participants did you find interesting?

2. What are the biggest challenges you see in your organization related to marketing and communications?

Chapter 2

Segmenting Your Audience

The first step to strategically creating effective marketing and communications content is to segment your audience. This process is covered in greater detail in the STP (Segmentation, Targeting & Positioning) Analysis portion of the NISM Strategic Planning book, but the following is a recap of segmentation and targeting, which is the natural next step.

Segmentation

Market segments are groups of people who have similar characteristics. These features might be needs, habits, or preferences and they could be associated to any number of common characteristics.

To begin segmenting your market, consider the following:

Demographics		Geography		Behavioral	
	Age		Country		
	Gender		Region		
	Marital status		State/Province		
	Ethnicity		City		
	Sexuality		County		
	Education		Neighborhood		
	Occupation				
	Income level				Product use
Psycho-graphics					Desired benefits
	Personality				Loyalty
	Risk aversion				
	Lifestyle				
	Values				

Once you have potential segments, begin qualifying each of them by researching their size, growth potential, accessibility, and saturation (how many competitors exist). Typically, organizations identify 2-3 segments to focus on, but that number will vary depending on your industry, product, and resources available to support your marketing efforts.

There's a helpful checklist for analyzing market segments in the first NISM textbook. We've included it here for your review.

When analyzing online market segments for social media, consider the following guidelines:

- *Use the STP process to more clearly define different customer and client groups, which will allow you to choose better targets for your products and services. This will, in turn, help you create clearer, more focused positioning that will achieve better results in social media.*
- *When segmenting your audience, think of your market as anyone who might be interested in your products or services and then group people or organizations together based on similarities.*
- *When defining segments, use common segmenting methodologies to help you group your segments. Methodologies you might use are demographics such as grouping by gender, age, income, region, and so forth, or by products if different products appeal to different types of customers.*
- *Use the same value propositions, keywords, and messages to people in the same segment because people and organizations in the same segment should have the same needs, and similar goals.*
- *Market to all members of the same segment in the same way, using the same channels and processes. For example, using blogs, microblog, or social networks.*
- *Use existing segment information to identify which segments new customers and organizations fit into.*

You can assess saturation by conducting a competitor analysis and systematically reviewing social media platforms and trending topics related to your industry. If you're interested in competitor analyses, they are explored in greater detail in *Social Media Project Management: Establish and Maintain Successful Projects & Campaigns*.

Targeting

Once you determine and qualify the segments associated with your market, you need to decide who to target. A clear picture of your options – your detailed list of characteristics that formed segments – has created the perfect environment for you to decide where to allocate your resources.

You may choose to target one or multiple segments and you may choose to weigh some segments more heavily than others. How will you decide? Ask yourself the following questions.

1. **Which group would be the most profitable for your organization?** If you're selling a luxury item and have to choose between two segments that seemed equally interested in a product, should you focus your resources equally? You might – but if you knew that one group had more disposable income, you would likely choose to focus on that group because it is more likely to be profitable for your organization.

2. **Which group is the biggest?** This consideration shouldn't be too surprising. The larger the group, the better the chances are that you'll capture a meaningful number of buyers. Your considerations are rarely this simple, but especially when testing a new product, it makes sense to go where the most people are.

3. **Where is there the most growth potential?** You're better off targeting a segment that is growing because that will mean you will continually have new people potentially interested in your product. This could refer to the

growth potential of the group – for example, if people with formal education are your target audience and formal education is increasing in popularity – or potential for product expansion within the group. Depending on your product, you might identify a segment interested in your current offering who are likely to be interested in products you have in development as well.

There are many considerations for targeting a segment, not the least of which is your gut feeling. If you're familiar with a product or industry, you've undoubtedly noticed patterns and seen successes and failures that can inform your decision.

Create a Market Map

Another way you can identify and categorize potential customers is a Market Map (also known as a Perceptual Map). It is a technique used by marketing professionals to visually depict the perceptions of current and potential customers. The company, brand, product line, or a specific product is depicted in contrast to the competition.

Strengths

A Market Map can help employees throughout an organization answer several critical questions.

1. Who are our customers?
2. Why are they interested in our product?
3. Where do they spend their time (both for marketing and purchasing considerations)?
4. How do they engage with our product?

A Market Map answers similar questions about the competition and can deepen an organization's understanding of a product.

1. Who are our competitors?
2. Why are customers interested in their product?
3. Where do your competitors and their customers spend their time?
4. How do they engage with our competitor's product?

Organizations across industries have found Market Maps useful in general, but particularly valuable in the following scenarios.

- Tracking the success and opportunities for a new product line or product
- Identifying changes in public perception
- Uncovering potential partnerships or related industries and interests
- Recovering from a negative event or a slow decline of interest

Weaknesses

As useful as Market Maps are, they are not perfect. Critics often claim that, since they typically only consider two of many possible variables, market maps can be too simplistic. While it's true that there is rarely a product with only two variables to consider when exploring a market, there are often at least two *primary* variables being explored at the current moment. The focus on just two considerations can often lead to a greater understanding of the consumer and potential opportunities.

How do you create a Market Map?

There are tools and websites like perceptualmaps.com that can help you create Market Maps, or you can create one from scratch using the following steps. To practice this skill, imagine you work for an organization that makes snack foods and you're exploring the idea of adding a granola bar to your product offering. In addition to keeping aligned with your brand, you also need to determine where your competitors are and why they chose those marketing options to identify your best product placement opportunities.

Once your Market Map is complete, it often becomes easy to see what attributes the current market values. In the following example, it's clear people prefer healthy and convenient snacks. Even at a glance, the market clearly demonstrates a preference.

1. Decide which product attributes you'd like to use. (These will eventually become your axes.) Choose attributes that will be very important to your market.

2. Name your map. It's no small task – you may create a few, so be specific and reference the axes and date created if possible. For example, you may wish to know how much your customers value health or convenience when it comes to snacks.

3. List your main competitors for the topic of the map. If you're creating a Market Map for a product, be careful not to list brand or line competitors that may not apply.

4. Create a scoring system that works with your attributes. You might have data available if your attribute is easily measured (price, for example) or you can create a simple 1-10 scale. If you create your measurement, you will also need to assign meaning to each number (e.g., 1 = low and 10 = high).

5. Draw a 4-square map, using your two attributes as axes, and add your scoring system.

Health and Convenience in Snack Foods (June 2017)

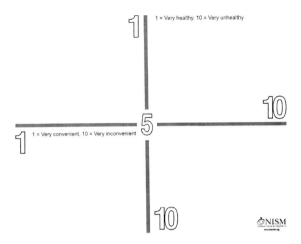

6. Assign scores to the competitors you listed in step 3. Depending on the attributes you've chosen, there are a variety of ways you could assign scores. In the example, we used a survey of 1,000 people who identified themselves as busy but health-conscious to determine how convenient each snack was and asked a nutrition expert to assign a health score.

7. Identify the market share of each competitor. Like the scoring in step 6, depending on the item, there are many approaches to identifying market share.

Competitor	Conv	Health	Market Share
Bananas	2	1	52%
Jake's Brand Trail Mix	5	3	27%
Hershey Chocolate Bar	3	10	3%
Bran Flakes (with milk)	9	2	11%

8. Plot each of the scores on your Market Map and add a bubble to represent the size of each item's market share.

The Importance of Health and Convenience in Snack Foods (June 2017)

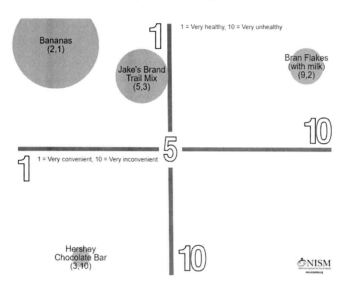

The findings of your Market Map exercise may not surprise you. Considering this example, would you think people wanted inconvenient and unhealthy snacks? Probably not. You probably would have guessed what this market map showed you – your competitors are making convenient, healthy snacks and so should you. But even if you don't uncover anything surprising, your map can still help you in other ways.

1. A Market Map can be used to get the non-marketing professionals on your team on board with your message quickly and easily. The results are often easy to interpret and memorable.
2. You might be surprised at the weight of influence of some attributes. For example, perhaps you guessed people preferred healthy snacks, but were surprised by the extent to which this was true.

Taking the time to really understand your audience is a critical first step to developing your strategic approach to marketing and communications. Even if you feel confident you understand your audience, it's a good idea to go through the steps of segmenting and even rethinking your targeting decisions. You never know what new and valuable markets might emerge with a second look.

Chapter 2 Discussion

1. What is the most influential psychographic information for your product, brand, or industry?

2. Create a Marketing Map related to your business.

   a. What two considerations did you choose and why?

   b. What did you learn by looking at what your competitors are doing?

   c. Who else in your organization would benefit from seeing this information, and what's the best way to share it with them?

Chapter 3

Creating a Communications Plan

A communications plan is used to help an organization create content and respond to others in a clear and consistent manner. It is beneficial even if your social media team only has one person because, whether they realize it or not, the organization's digital presence is every employee's responsibility to some degree. Every person connected to an organization can support the brand in their own way. With guidelines for consistent messaging, their support can have the maximum amount of positive influence.

A communications plan is helpful in a number of ways.

- If the social media strategy is managed by one person or a small team, but there are multiple teams throughout the organization that contribute content and are active online, a communications plan can help everyone move quickly and confidently toward the same goals.
- An organization whose employees learn to follow a communications plan have a greater chance of brand consistency, no matter the situation (planned event, positive feedback, customer complaint, etc.).
- Everyone in the organization can support events, promotions, and real-time happenings easily – and the easier something is to do, the more likely people are to do it.
- If an employee panics, they are more likely to make a difficult situation worse. Clear guidelines for handling negative feedback or conversations about product

difficulties on social media can decrease the stress of the situation and reduce the risk of escalation from an inappropriate response.

- When new employees, consultants, or vendors join the organization, they can quickly join the online conversation and begin promoting the brand through their own channels and creative ideas.

Components of a Communications Plan

The details of a communications plan will vary between organizations. Social media professionals should carefully consider the unique challenges and opportunities that are likely to emerge within their business or industry when creating their specific plan, but the following guide can be applied to any organization as a framework.

- First, identify the overarching information everyone participating needs to know. This typically includes a brief overview of the organization, its guiding principles, and a general description of the tactics used online to ensure effective and consistent brand promotion from the whole of your team.
- Second, drill down and explain how the brand can be supported on individual platforms. This information is influenced by the overarching details but provides specific guidance for *how* individuals should engage online. For example, a guiding principle in your organization may be to respond to comments, but those responses look different on every social media platform, with different limitations and opportunities. An individual would first understand that, as an organization, two-way conversations are valued and that they should engage. They could then look for guidance on using a specific social media tool in the most effective way.

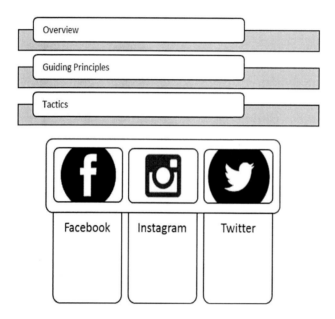

Sample Communications Plan

The following is a sample communications plan that could be modified for any organization. Details specific to the organization's goals and approach to maintaining their digital presence would need to be added, but the overall design, length, and language should be applicable for most organizations. Also, we randomly selected three social media sites to demonstrate how platforms should be described and how that might overlap. Depending on what platforms your organization focuses on, you may need to add or remove specific descriptions. Each platform you utilize should be clearly represented in your communications plan.

Overview

We recognize that our digital presence is important to the success of our organization and that you – our community – are the greatest contributors to that success. Through our social media, we have the opportunity to reach new audience members every day and share the resources and opportunities we have to offer.

Our social media channels are not the only way we connect with our community, and this communications plan is part of a larger strategy that includes strategic partnerships <list if applicable>, traditional advertising <list if applicable> and sponsorships <list if applicable>. We cross-promote these communication tools on all channels to improve our ability to serve our current customer base and attract new customers who could benefit from our services.

Guiding Principles

Our goal is to continually provide information to our community that educates and inspires. We invite our community members to engage with us on our social platforms by contributing their own comments and sharing what we post, and by tagging us in their conversations. To the extent possible, we respond to all comments and questions.

Tactics

On each platform, we use the following tactics to uphold our guiding principles.

1. **Be honest and positive.** If a situation involving the organization does not allow us to be transparent (typically for legal or ethical reasons), share to the extent possible and be honest about the limitation.
2. **In all communications, be professional.** While we want the tone on each platform to be friendly, it is important to remember that you are still representing the organization.
3. **Identify yourself.** When managing a platform as a group, add your initials or first name at the end of your

post. It's a great way to connect with followers on a more personal level.

4. **Share content that is of high quality and truthful.** Remember that content we create and content we share should enhance our brand.

5. **Do not value quantity over quality.** It is tempting to flood social media channels with information, but that increases the chances that you will share content that isn't valuable and it may alienate your followers if they feel you're clogging their newsfeed.

6. **Before sharing, verify the accuracy of information to the furthest extent possible.** It's possible that, even with due diligence, you might share incorrect information, but for every topic – no matter how insignificant it may seem – the content should be verified as accurate to the extent possible.

7. **Post at times when your community is active on that platform.** This will vary by platform, but pay attention to when your community is online. Also, don't miss opportunities to be more active during events that might cause your community members to be online at unusual times.

8. **Err on the side of caution.** If you think a post might be offensive, don't post it.

9. **Apologize if you make a mistake.** If you do post content that is offensive to a member of your community or is later proven to be false, apologize to the community and do what is needed to make amends.

10. **Promote our successes, not our competitors' failures.** Except in the case of promoting necessary awareness (e.g., a food recall or other safety concern) do not engage in conversations that disparage our competition. Rather, focus on our successes.

11. **Talk to followers.** If people engage with us on any platform, respond! Conversations with current and potential customers should be fun and relaxed. Provide

support when needed, resolve issues as they arise, but otherwise use the social media platforms as a place to connect with our community.

12. **Listen to followers.** Even if they don't directly ask for a change, pay attention to what they value and how we could make changes to better serve them.

Facebook

```
< Link to Facebook Page >
```

What is Facebook?

Facebook is a social networking site people use to keep in touch with friends and family around the world. Typical posts include video, photos, links to articles, and original personal content (e.g., "Happy Birthday, Paige" or "I passed my SMS exam today!"). Users choose which profiles (people) and pages (organizations) they'd like to follow. People are likely to see the posts generated by the people and pages they are following, though Facebook uses an algorithm to determine exactly who sees what, so a follower is not guaranteed to see every post.

Audience

According to Pew Research Center:

"79% of internet users (68% of all U.S. adults) use Facebook.

"Roughly eight-in-ten online Americans (79%) now use Facebook, a 7-percentage-point increase from a survey conducted at a similar point in 2015.

"Young adults continue to report using Facebook at high rates, but older adults are joining in increasing numbers. Some 62% of online adults ages 65 and older now use Facebook, a 14-point increase from the 48% who reported doing so in 2015. In addition, women continue to use Facebook at somewhat higher rates than men: 83% of female

internet users and 75% of male internet users are Facebook adopters."

< If available and applicable, it is beneficial to add specific details about your Facebook audience here. Details may include the number of followers, typical engagement and any demographics you have available (found on your insights page). >

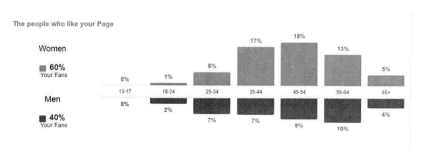

The people who like your Page

Tips
We have found the content that receives the most engagement on Facebook to be the following:
< include any additional content – the more specific the better – you have found your audience responds to >

- Video
- Live video
- High-quality images
- Relevant articles
- Any original educational content

Additionally, consider the following tips when posting:

- **Tag people or organizations associated with the post.** This will increase your reach and likely lead to them engaging with you.

- **Respond to people who engage with your post.** Answer questions or just join in a fun conversation as each situation dictates.
- **Search for relevant news posts on a daily basis.** If the headline doesn't make it obvious, share why you believe they will enjoy the post. Know what content interests your audience and share it.
- **Highlight news about the organization.** If a news outlet shares a story about us or our community, we want to help it go viral online!

Instagram

<Link to Instagram Account>

What is Instagram?

Instagram is a mobile photo and video-sharing social networking platform that encourages users to take pictures and videos, and share them either publicly or privately through their app. Instagram is committed to helping users enjoy the moment by supporting real-time photo sharing as opposed to sharing articles or organizational information.

Audience

According to Pew Research Center:

"32% of internet users (28% of all U.S. adults) use Instagram.

"Around one-third of online adults (32%) report using Instagram – roughly the same share as in 2015, when 27% of online adults did so.

"To a greater extent than the other social platforms measured in this survey, Instagram use is especially high among younger adults. Roughly six-in-ten online adults ages 18-29 (59%) use Instagram, nearly double the share among 30- to 49-year-olds (33%) and more than seven times the share

among those 65 and older (8%). And as was the case in previous Pew Research Center surveys of social media use, female internet users are more likely to use Instagram than men (38% vs. 26%)."

< If available and applicable, it is beneficial to add specific details about your Instagram audience here. Business accounts have an insights page with this information available, so if you haven't already switched to a business account, we highly recommend doing so. Details may include the number of followers, typical engagement, and any demographics you have available. >

Tips

< include any additional content – the more specific the better – you have found your audience responds to. >

Consider the following tips when posting:

- **Tag people or organizations associated with the picture.** This will increase your reach and likely lead to them engaging with you.
- **Respond to people who engage with your post.** Answer questions or just join in a fun conversation as each situation dictates.
- **Take interesting pictures.** Instagram is the perfect place to let your creativity loose! Instead of snapping a traditional team picture, tilt the camera and take action shots. Let your artistic side show if you see something that would make a unique image.
- **Share your Instagram photos on other platforms.** With one click, your Instagram photo can be shared on multiple platforms outside of Instagram. You easily can get more mileage out of each photo. (Follow the recommended guidelines for those platforms.)
- **Use Instagram Takeovers.** Invite a person or organization to take over your Instagram account for the day.

Not only will it energize your account by providing new and interesting content, you're also likely to pick up new followers associated with whoever took over your account.

- **Support partners and complementary businesses.** Engage with partners and those who support your mission by commenting on their photos and tagging them in relevant posts.

Twitter

```
< Link to Twitter Profile >
```

What is Twitter?

Twitter is a news and networking platform where users post messages that are a maximum of 140 characters. The posts are called tweets and can contain text, images, or links. Twitter is notorious for brief posts and a fast-moving feed.

Audience

According to Pew Research Center:

"24% of internet users (21% of all U.S. adults) use Twitter.

"Roughly one-quarter of online adults (24%) use Twitter, a proportion that is statistically unchanged from a survey conducted in 2015 (23%).

"Younger Americans are more likely than older Americans to be on Twitter. Some 36% of online adults ages 18-29 are on the social network, more than triple the share among online adults ages 65 and older (just 10% of whom are Twitter users).

"Twitter is also somewhat more popular among the highly educated: 29% of internet users with college degrees use

Twitter, compared with 20% of those with high school degrees or less."

<If available and applicable, it is beneficial to add specific details about your Twitter audience here. Details may include the number of followers, typical engagement and any demographics you have available (found on your analytics tab).>

Tips

<Include any additional content – the more specific the better – you have found your audience responds to.>

Consider the following tips when posting:

- **Keep your message short.** By design, you can't post more than 140 characters in a tweet anyway, but the shorter the tweet the more likely you are to receive engagement. The recommended length is about 100 characters.

- **Tag people or organizations associated with the post.** This will increase your reach and likely lead to them engaging with you.

- **Use popular hashtags.** Look to see what's trending and add that hashtag to your posts to join active conversations. Trending hashtags are listed on Twitter (under the trends tab or on the main screen, depending on the device you're using) or you can use search engines to look for active hashtags. You can also use existing hashtags on a regular basis (like #Motivation-Monday) that are related to the content you're posting to connect with potential new followers.

- **Create a new hashtag.** You don't have to join an existing conversation – you can start one! If you have an event or topic that's unique, create a hashtag and include it in your tweets. That way people can find any related messages by following the hashtag. When creating your hashtag, remember to make it as short as possible and easy to remember – avoid any tricky spellings or complicated words.
- **Respond to people who tag you or retweet your message.** Ask or answer questions, thank them, or just join in a fun conversation as each situation dictates.
- **Search for relevant news posts on a daily basis.** Identify news and content relating to <Briefly highlight what content interests your audience> and share it throughout the day.
- **Retweet news about the organization often.** Remember, Twitter feeds move quickly. If a news outlet shares a story about us or our community, we want to share it several times throughout the day.

A detailed communications plan is an excellent way to keep everyone supporting your organization on the same page. It makes communicating online easy and ensures your message will have the greatest reach. If anyone asks you why the organization needs a communications plan or questions why you follow it so strictly, relay the following points.

With a communications plan:

- **You'll save time.** Staff can be brought into the social media workflow more quickly with less direction. In real-time, you'll also be able to respond to your community more quickly.
- **The quality of your responses will be better.** The more clearly your team understands your mission and message, the better their responses will be. And your staff will be better equipped to handle challenging situations.
- **Your branding will remain consistent.** A communications plan will help you maintain a consistent organizational voice and pattern of response.
- **You'll stay aligned with the organization's strategic goals.** With a communications plan, you're less likely to follow a shiny object and drift away from your organizational message.

Chapter 3 Discussion

1. Who would benefit from seeing your organization's communications plan? Consider internal and external individuals and groups who support you and your message.

2. If your organization has a communications plan, note what changes you would recommend. And if your organization doesn't have a communications plan, use this chapter as a guide to create one.

Part Two
Gauge Audience Interest

Chapter 4

Working with Your Core Audience

When creating content for public platforms, you can't prevent specific people from seeing your content, but there are things you can do to ensure the people you want to connect with see what you share. Those people you're most interested in are known as your *core audience* and here are a few tips to help you get the most out of your relationship with them.

Who is your core audience?

Especially when a business is new, there is often a feeling – or even a stated goal – of reaching as many people as possible with a marketing message. Wild marketing stunts, viral videos, and beautifully designed infographics that target a wide audience can be a great way to increase your brand recognition, but it's also important to identify your core audience – the people who will actually purchase your products and promote your brand – since they will ultimately be the group who sustains your business.

You might be able to identify your core audience without much thought. Some brands have an obvious core group of people loyal to the brand and its messaging. However, it's always a good idea to check in on a routine basis to make sure your core audience hasn't changed. Here are a few questions you could ask yourself to make sure you are still on track.

1. Have we launched any new products or engaged in any new initiatives that might attract a new core audience?

2. Have we made any changes that might alienate some or all of the core audience we have currently identified?

3. When reviewing platform analytics, are there any changes in our engagement demographics? If so, do we know why and if the change is likely temporary or permanent?

4. Have our competitors, strategic partners, or complementary businesses begun to target new audiences? If so, does it make sense for us to do the same?

These questions and any others you think will help you gain insight into your core audience may indicate that your strategic approach is still solid and no changes are needed. It might also indicate that you have new opportunities to explore. Either way, it is worth the time it takes to check in on your current audience.

Why is your core audience so important?

This may seem obvious, but it's important enough to spell it out. Your core audience is the group of consumers tied to your organization's financial success. Whether you are a government, for-profit, or non-profit group, funding is important. Your core audience is made up of the people who:

- Buy your product/service
- Approve the purchase of your product/service
- Advocate for/Legitimize your organization

Without these key players, the most creative marketing in the world won't keep your doors open. You need sales, investors, and/or continuing support from governing bodies if you want to keep your business running. It isn't enough to be popular; you must have the support of the right people.

What does your core audience respond to?

When you begin creating material for your core audience, you'll have to rely on a certain amount of trial and error. With research and common sense, you can put together a pretty accurate list of what your core audience will respond to, but over time you have the advantage of observing what they really appreciate. To identify what they value, you can certainly ask them to share ideas, which will also increase their buy-in by allowing them to contribute to the content shared by the organization. But monitoring their actions is even more telling.

Here are a few observations NISM social media strategists observed. Can you relate to any of them?

- *"My community never liked, shared, or commented on articles about how they could improve their business, and yet those posts had the highest click-through rate. I realized the community members valued the content, but they didn't want to admit to needing help. That realization helped me understand how I could better support the community by providing opportunities for people to get help and advice anonymously."*
- *"My budget finally allowed me to hire a professional photographer and I couldn't believe how quickly engagement increased. I asked a few community members if they had noticed anything different and they each said something like 'it seems like you've been posting more...' I think the better pictures caught their attention. I was reminded that my audience is very active on social media and that means I'm competing with a lot of noise. I'm focusing on catchy headlines next and I bet it has the same effect."*
- *"Whenever I posted 'how to' posts, I got a ton of engagement, but I never saw any change in the behavior of the community. I researched how many people were actually clicking on the article – not just liking the*

post – and found the percentage was shockingly low. In some cases, no one had opened the article even though it had received a ton of likes and shares! I wanted to help my readers, so I began posting interesting pieces of the article on each platform with the link. That got their attention and the number of click-throughs skyrocketed!"

What your audience does or doesn't respond to doesn't matter as long as you know what gets their attention. Observe and, where possible, measure what leads to engagement and strategically apply what you have learned to all of your messaging.

Chapter 4 Discussion

1. Assess at least three platforms where your audience is active. Note what types of content they respond to and any other information that you believe may have influenced their activity.

2. Identify at least two people within your organization – any position and any level – you have never talked to about the organization's audience. Ask them to share their opinion about who your core audience is and what they are likely to respond to. Compare their ideas to the work you're already doing and note any potential opportunities that emerge.

3. After reviewing the above information about your audience, brainstorm 3-5 ways you might make small adjustments to your social media posts in order to test additional engagement opportunities.

Chapter 5

Audience Engagement

Understanding how your audience prefers to engage with you will help you position your content in the most appealing and therefore most effective ways. For example, if you work in the fitness industry and you know your audience loves sharing their accomplishments, providing a way for them to share their success stories is a smart way to boost engagement.

Engagement isn't always initially fun and positive, of course. A social media professional may engage with community members for many different reasons.

- Positive experiences and feedback
- Negative experiences and feedback
- Neutral experiences and feedback
- Questions or recommendations about the product
- Complaints

Another layer of consideration for each engagement is who is contributing the feedback. Whether the content is from a known community member, an influencer, or is anonymous, it should be given consideration – but the sender and any intent you can infer should influence how you handle the engagement. Ask yourself the following questions:

1. **Is the content genuine and positive?** If it is, you have a great opportunity to engage with the audience member by asking them to share more, responding specifically to their comments, or even just by thanking them.

2. **Is their feedback – even if it seems negative – genuinely helpful?** When I read a review for clothing and it says, "These pants are too long! I had to have them hemmed," I am *more* likely to purchase the product than I was before I read the review. I prefer pants that are too long for most people. What some might perceive as a negative review is actually very beneficial to the community. If they shared feedback in a respectful manner, see if you can turn it into a positive – maybe thank them for their feedback.

Says an egg with 21 followers. #troll

Fathers Initiative @Norsewolfe
@aravosis not true. Who says she won by 2.2 mil? The mainstream media? The media is nothing more than a Communist Style 1-party system

7:18 PM - 26 Nov 2016

3. **Is the sender an identified troll?** The tweet below is an example of how trolls can, in some cases, be identified very quickly. The topic (politics) is especially vulnerable to trolls and the respondent quickly recognized that a Twitter account without a profile picture (that's the egg reference) and 21 followers is likely a fake or temporary account created to troll. If you do identify a troll, you may choose to respond, but in most cases, it's best to ignore them.

4. **Is it a rant or a joke?** Like an identified troll, there's no one right way to handle someone who has involved your brand in a rant or joke, but identifying their intent to the best of your ability may help you craft your response

– or solidify your decision not to respond. It's important to remember the absence of tone and the ability people have to quickly, easily, and often thoughtlessly post content.

It can be intimidating to respond to an angry – or even slightly irritated – customer who's started a potentially dangerous conversation on a very public platform. We've all heard the stories of customers who become an internet sensation because of their rant on social media. We've also heard about the employees who fired back, forgoing professionalism and typically losing their jobs. What can we do to remain active, engage with our customers in a meaningful way, and remain positive? The following are examples of companies who have taken unique approaches to engagement and have accepted the challenges.

The Mysterious Package Company

The Mysterious Package Company describes itself on its Facebook page in the following way:

"The Mysterious Package Company provides unique and custom-made gifts delivered by mail, and wrapped in a handcrafted experience unlike any other. Custom made crates, letters and telegrams from long-lost relatives, and seemingly innocuous newspaper clippings add a richness to the curious goods contained within. Each experience is uniquely tailored to each person.

"We are a members-only service. Membership is free, but you must fill in our application form in order to be considered as a member. We are more than simply a way to send packages, we are a community of like-minded people who believe that life needs to be less mundane.

"An application does not guarantee membership.

"It is the policy of The Mysterious Package Company to neither confirm nor deny our involvement with any specific packages. That would be telling."

This entertainment company has several unique challenges associated with engaging users. The first is the balance of information. When you're trying to be mysterious, sharing too much about what you're offering undercuts the value of your product. But if you don't share enough, the right people won't be interested.

The second unique challenge is that the value of the product itself is highly subjective. As an organization, they are at risk of bad reviews if their mysteries are too difficult to solve or if they are too easy – determinations that are different from person to person.

However, The Mysterious Package Company does an excellent job of balancing both. The following examples demonstrate a few opportunities and challenges a lot of organizations can likely relate to.

Repetitive Questions

If you feel like you answer the same questions over and over again on social media, you are not alone. You have to resist the urge to say, "Is there some reason you didn't look for this on our website?" You must also keep your posts interesting for others who visit your sites.

Take a look at this post from The Mysterious Package Company, a few of their customer questions, and how the organization responded.

The Mysterious Package Company
November 10 at 12:15pm ·

They say there is no honour among thieves, and in many cases that is true.
In the early 18th century, the most disreputable dregs ever to sail the seas
carry out an impressive heist together.

It is with great excitement that we announce our latest experience: The Lost
Treasure of John Augur, a premium pirate adventure on the high seas,
where you or an unsuspecting loved one become a part of the story.
Exclusively for members only, so apply now!

The Lost Treasure of John Augur
Neil Patrick Harris, actor and member since 2016: "It chilled me to my core.
Absolutely stellar in every way."
MYSTERIOUSPACKAGE.COM

Questions like these fill the company's Facebook page.
Many people could have their questions answered simply by
scrolling through what others had recently written. And The
Mysterious Package Company could have relied on people
doing that to get their answers, but they didn't. They wrote a
unique response for each customer.

What do their responses do for their brand and community? By responding to even the most basic, repetitive questions, they have clearly demonstrated that their customers are
important to them. That person who was interested enough
to ask a question now feels connected because they got a
response. And even if that specific person doesn't become
a customer, the hundreds and thousands of others who post
could now have a more positive perception of the organization.

Steph Stroble You can only get the tshirt and coin if you sign up now? 😕 I want the whole experience but I don't want the first shipment to be lost in the hullabaloo of the holiday!! Can I order now to receive the tshirt and coin, but delay shipping until January?

Like · Reply · ⬤ 1 · November 10 at 2:52pm

> 🏷 **The Mysterious Package Company** Certainly. Email Member Services at concierge@mysteriouspackage.com immediately after your order, and let them know when you wish your experience to begin.
>
> Like · Reply · ⬤ 1 · November 10 at 3:43pm

 Amber Johanna Serradimigni During the holiday season, is lead time on your shipment delayed? When would be a good time to request an experience to be delivered approximately the week of Christmas?

Like · Reply · November 10 at 1:14pm

> 🏷 **The Mysterious Package Company** Any experience ordered prior to the end of November will see at least their first mailing arrive before Christmas (in North America only). The Lost Treasure of John Augur will have the first mailing scheduled to ship so it should arrive prior to Christmas, going out around the middle of December.
>
> Like · Reply · ⬤ 2 · November 10 at 1:17pm

It should also be noted that by responding on this specific platform (Facebook), the organization is keeping their post alive. The more they and others contribute, the more likely the post is to appear and reappear in feeds.

The Complisult

Have you ever read a message from someone and wondered if they were complimenting or insulting you? It's what we like to call a complisult – half compliment, half insult. (E.g., "It's great to see you finally included recent research!") They appear most often on social media pages when audience members are feeling passive-aggressive, if they want to complain without hurting your feelings, or if they're trying to be funny. However they emerge, they can be tricky to manage.

First, watch for trolls. If someone is trying to bait you, don't fall for it. Second, honestly ask yourself if their feedback is valid. If it is, share it with your team as appropriate. If it isn't, don't waste your energy worrying about it. Just because someone has an opinion that is different from yours doesn't mean their opinion is right.

While each situation is different, a safe approach is to stick with the facts whenever possible. Always be kind, but if someone has accused you unjustly and you can prove it, share the correct information with them. If you have determined they're providing you with genuine feedback, you'll likely get a very positive reply. And if they're right, acknowledge it and thank them for the feedback. You may not want or be able to share details, but you don't have to. Simply acknowledging their contribution is often enough.

A Complaint

What if there is no bright side? What if the post is just a complaint and the customer doesn't want a resolution – they want a public sounding board?

Steve Spurr DON'T switch. Worst customer service on the planet.
Like · Reply · 5 · 1 hr

Sprint Steve Spurr - This is not good to see. We'd like to assist you with your concerns. Please, send us a Private Message with your 6-10 digit security PIN. You can send us a Private Message by clicking "Message" in our page. We await your response. - Greg S
Like · Reply · 1 hr
↳ View more replies

Lesa Gladstone Please tell me why I have waited 1 month for the return kit for my IPhone 6s, 5 1/2 hours of talk time on the phone with "Customer Care" and my account is still screwed up and I still do not have my return kit for my IPhone 6s after doing my upgrade? M... See More
Like · Reply · 1 · 1 hr
↳ View previous replies

Sprint Hi Larry, this isn't the type of feedback we like to receive from our customers. Can you please elaborate on the issue you're having. W await your response. - ChristianW
Like · Reply · 1 hr
↳ View more replies

There are a lot of industries where this is prevalent. Restaurants, cell phone providers, and cable companies all seem to generate more complaints on their social media sites than positive comments. Why do they bother?

1. It's suspicious for an organization to not be on social media. In today's world, it's practically a requirement to be present on most of the major platforms.
2. If customers can't complain on a platform you provide, they'll find a different place to post their concerns. At least on your platform, you can more easily manage the feedback.
3. Feedback from angry customers isn't always all bad. Sometimes by acknowledging their concerns, you can convert an angry customer to a loyal one.
4. By allowing complaints, you have the opportunity to demonstrate a level of professionalism that most consumers will appreciate. Even if you can't fix the specific problem the customer you're working with is having, your approach to a challenging situation might be exactly what another customer is looking for.

It may seem like constantly reacting to customer feedback on social media would be stressful. In fact, that's what leads to a lot of small business owners giving up on managing their own digital presence. They approach every situation as if it's new and are quickly exhausted. To avoid that result, remember the following when engaging with your audience.

1. Include engagement in your strategic plan. If you make it part of moving organizational initiatives forward, you're more likely to get support from others in the organization as needed.
2. Make as much of the process as possible a routine. Check your platforms at roughly the same times throughout the day, respond with a consistent voice,

and divide responsibilities among teammates when possible.

3. Use a communications plan to help more people throughout the organization engage with the audience in a consistent manner.

4. Look for opportunities to learn from each engagement and try not to take any of them – especially the trolls – personally. Oftentimes a thoughtful acknowledgement can diffuse a situation quickly.

Chapter 5 Discussion

1. Assess engagement on at least two of your social media platforms. Why do your customers typically engage with you? What motivates them to respond to your posts – either positively or negatively?

2. Considering what motivates them to respond, how can you make the most out of their engagement?

Part Three
Create the Best Content

Chapter 6

What Do Your Customers Value?

E very social media strategist faces the same question: What will interest my audience? The answer is different for every business and within every business it will continually change. New ideas and opportunities create fickle audience members with limited attention spans – but you can connect with them by identifying trends and remaining agile in your planning.

The following is a list of trends we've seen recently. At the time of this writing, some are just getting started, others have hit their stride, and still more are beginning to fade. Each will also vary in popularity depending on industry, but they all made enough of an impact in recent history that they should be considered by your organization.

Video

2016 was called "the year of video" by many. Some platforms increased promotion of their video feature by adding filters and enhancements. Instagram and Snapchat, for example, have obviously recognized the value of storytelling through video. They've steadily been improving and promoting options for users and their audience is embracing the changes.

Facebook Live
In August of 2015, Facebook launched Facebook Live, which allowed users to broadcast live video streams and their followers to comment in real-time. The idea was well-received,

though initially users seemed to struggle with the fear of live broadcasting. Facebook responded with campaigns focused on helping people understand how easy it was to do and, steadily, the technique gained popularity. For professional users, there was a great appeal because everything is created in real-time, so it's incredibly efficient. Using Facebook Live at trade shows, product demos, or even to just talk with customers might be somewhat risky – it is live, after all, and you don't always know what's going to happen – but the ease of use more than makes up for the risk.

Challenges with Video

Time and resources are the two most commonly cited challenges associated with implementing a robust video plan. As technology becomes more accessible (easier to use and less expensive), these challenges lessen. However, social media professionals can manage some of these difficulties by carefully considering how video fits into their strategic plan. Should room be made in the budget to hire a freelance videographer? Should continuing education dollars be allocated to learning more about creating video or about video on specific platforms? Deciding this early is one of the best ways you can set yourself up for success.

Top Ten Video Tips

Whether you're an expert or new to working with live or pre-recorded video, review these tips! We've collected the most common themes from social media professionals, marketers, educators, and business professionals. Here's what they say:

1. **Craft a good title.** If you put time and energy into creating an amazing video, but the title isn't interesting enough to catch anyone's attention, all your work may have been for nothing! Consider what will make your video stand out – but make sure the title also describes the content well enough to attract the right audience.

2. **Invest in editing software – and learn how to use it.** There are so many options, you're guaranteed to find something that will work for your budget. Most importantly, once you choose your software, learn how to use it. Simple techniques like transitions and text on the screen can make a tremendous difference in how well your video is received.

3. **Keep it short.** Depending on your topic and platform, there are recommended maximum lengths for videos. Consider your topic, audience, and platform and create videos accordingly. If you feel you need more time, you can always create multiple videos – but first try to be more succinct.

4. **Brand your content.** Related to the second recommendation, a common missed opportunity is branding your video. Include your logo, website, contact information, etc. whenever you can (without decreasing the value of the video) to help viewers keep your brand top of mind.

5. **Share on as many platforms as possible.** You might create a video with the intention of sharing it on Facebook or YouTube, but don't limit yourself. If you post a video on YouTube, for example, you now have a link. That means you can easily share it on all your other platforms, add it to your email signature, or include it in your newsletter. Posting the initial copy of your video is just the beginning.

6. **Inform without selling.** You don't have to tell people they need to buy your product – you can show them how your product will make their life better. If you connect with them as a subject matter expert genuinely interested in making their life better, you have the opportunity to make a meaningful connection with them that converts to a sale.

7. **Add description and tags.** Depending on where you're sharing your video, you probably have the opportunity to add meaningful text – keywords, a description,

transcript, etc. Don't skip this step – it's how people will find your video! Wherever you are posting, take a moment to read the recommendations provided by the platform to make sure you don't miss any opportunities to help people find your content.

8. **Include a call to action.** What do you want people to do before, during, after or as a result of watching your video? Tell them! Keep your direction short and simple, but be clear about what their next action should be. Video is a great way to increase traffic to your website or to encourage people to share their information – and you can increase your chances of making a meaningful connection by providing clear direction.

9. **Answer a question or shatter a myth.** One of the most popular uses for video is problem-solving. How do I create a Thanksgiving centerpiece? What's the best way to increase traffic to my new website? Questions like these can certainly be answered in an article, but more and more people are looking for their solutions on video – especially if any kind of demonstration is deemed to be helpful. An opportunity to create an educational video that goes viral is to shatter a myth related to your area of expertise. Do you offer environmentally friendly cleaning services? Show how a solution anyone can make in their kitchen is more powerful than a store-bought product. Do you offer a service that helps employees stay focused at work? Interview people in an office space and share their feedback about just how hard they *aren't* working when they stay late in the office. Taking something we believe or take for granted and proving it wrong – ideally while your brand provides a solution – is a great way to capture the attention of your ideal customer.

10. **Plan, but don't be too scripted.** Over the last decade, we've seen consumer opinion shift. Where there used

to be an increase in trust and perception of professionalism associated with high-quality, carefully scripted video, people are now responding more positively to unscripted video because – whether it's true or not – the perception is that it's more honest. So, if you have the option of having your CEO read a message from a teleprompter or recording the message she delivers at the Monday morning staff meeting, you might choose the latter. Don't publish content filled with verbal pauses and unnecessary footage, but don't undervalue how endearing imperfections can be.

Microblogging

Microblogging – short, frequent posts on sites like Twitter – continues to be a popular social media technique. While many people struggle initially to speak so concisely, once you learn a few success tips, most people find microblogging to be a fun and effective way to participate in fast-paced conversations.

Certified Social Media Strategist and NISM instructor Lisa Flowers shared some of her Twitter tips – many of which are applicable on other microblogging platforms. If you'd like to connect with Lisa and check out how she runs her Twitter page, you can follow her at @LisaLFlowers.

It's important to note that this list is written quite appropriately as short, meaningful text. Notice how differently it reads and yet how clear the content is.

Why use Twitter?

1. You don't need to be famous.
2. You don't need a huge following before you can start seeing results.
3. You don't need to pay for advertising.

4. Twitter has become a powerful channel for branding, influence, authority, digital diplomacy, news, and even scandal.
5. It's a great way to connect, discover, and learn.
6. You can follow ANYONE – in the WORLD!
7. And talk to them.
8. And see what they are talking about.
9. And see who they are talking to.
10. And be part of their conversation.
11. Or start a conversation!

Twitter can help you:

- Generate traffic to your website or blog
- Connect to influencers
- Connect to potential customers
- Start conversations or take part in conversations
- Build brand recognition
- Find information
- Help your sales
- Gain influence
- Be seen as a thought leader or expert
- Have fun!

Twitter Chat Tips

A Twitter chat is a conversation on Twitter organized around a specific topic using a designated hashtag to keep everyone in the same conversation. The host of the chat will pose questions (using Q1, Q2, etc.) and participants respond (using A1, A2, etc.). Twitter chats are a great way to meet new people on Twitter and learn valuable information.

Pre-Chat

- Think about the topic before the chat.

- Write down thoughtful questions and answers before the chat. This can save you a lot of time!
- Follow the host and guest on Twitter.
- Consider following other participants before the chat and letting them know you look forward to seeing them there.

During the Chat

- Be sure to include the chat hashtag in every tweet.
- The tweet chat host will use "Q" and the number for each question.
- When you respond or answer the Q, mark it with A (for answer) and the number of the original question so other participants can link your response with the correct question.
   Here's an example:
   Q2: What is your favorite color? #TwitterChat17
   A2: Purple

Engage Other Chat Participants

- Like or retweet their tweets.
- Chat with them (using the hashtag) during the chat. Let them know you like their tweet.
- Don't over-promote, but do use the chat to highlight your expertise, share knowledge about the topic, etc.
- If your recent blog post, upcoming event, or services can provide value to people in the chat and relate to the conversation, mention it in your tweets.

Post Chat

- Follow up after the tweet chat. If others retweeted your tweet, thank them.

- Offer compliments to other participants, the host and guest.
- You'll probably meet new people and get new followers through the tweet chat. Introduce yourself and follow them back.
- Follow the people behind those tweets and keep the chat/conversation going!
- If you enjoyed the chat, tweet that you will see everyone next week or whenever the next chat is scheduled.

My Secret Tool on Twitter – Lists

What is a list?

A list is a curated group of Twitter accounts. You can create your own lists or subscribe to lists created by others. Viewing a list timeline will show you a stream of Tweets from only the accounts on that list.

- You can see who is subscribing to your Twitter lists.
- You can see what lists you are a member of.
- You can edit/delete your created lists at any time.
- You can subscribe to other people's lists.
- You can search for Twitter lists to follow.
- Include yourself in the lists you make.
- Want to be considered a thought leader in your industry?

  ○ Add yourself to a Twitter list of thought leaders.

- Want to increase your Twitter followers and engagement?

○ Add yourself to the most popular lists you've created (if it makes sense to do so).

There are a few tactical tricks to being successful on Twitter – using sites like bit.ly to shorten website links, text shorthand (i.e., "B4 u go" instead of "before you go") to save character space, and sharing images to make your tweets stand out. As a social media strategist, you have to learn the tactical skills you need to post on platforms – and you have to keep up with the changes!

Using Event Hashtags

The last time you had an event – a product launch, a grand opening, etc. – did you strategically choose event hashtags to help you reach your audience? By following a few simple steps, hashtags can help you start a conversation with your audience or tap into existing topics your industry is already buzzing about!

Event Hashtags

Hashtags are used on many platforms, so they deserve special consideration every time you have an event or product launch.

Here are a few tips to follow:

Bring people together.

Create a unique hashtag and share it with your group on all invitations and social media campaign materials.

Join a popular discussion.

What are people in your industry talking about?

Join the conversation by asking questions and sharing information!

Daily Hashtags

Day of the Week #TBT

Industry Term #socialmedia

Popular #quotes

Trending Remember to search for hashtags that are trending!

Graphics and Infographics

On all platforms, well-crafted graphics and infographics continue to be successful. There is so much activity online, it isn't surprising that a crisp image is one of the things users are most likely to stop for. Graphics and especially infographics are appealing because they typically provide important and interesting information in an easy-to-read format that busy people appreciate.

Top Ten Graphics Tips

We've collected the most common themes from social media professionals, marketers, educators, and business professionals. Like video, there are definitely best practices that can help your graphics and infographics stand out. In fact, some of the recommendations that apply to video also apply to graphics.

It's also important to remember that this isn't a simple task – it takes research, practice, and talent. There are many professionals who create graphics for a living. Consider your team and the skill sets you have access to – you might choose to hire a freelancer or external organization to help you create the best possible images for your marketing strategy.

1. **Use numbers.** Think of some of your favorite infographics. What do they have in common? For most people, numbers (statistics, recommendations, counts) are really helpful. Whatever content you're talking about, if you can include numbers, you should!

2. **Craft a good title.** The design and flow of your graphic is probably what will catch the eye of your reader, but a good title can help them understand what content is in the graphic and how it can help them. Don't be too clever – it's important they immediately understand what the content is. But don't be boring, either. If

you've created a beautiful graphic, you should take the time to create an equally beautiful title.

3. **Invest in high quality images.** Are you creating graphics in Microsoft PowerPoint? It certainly works, but sites like Piktochart and Canva help social media strategists create amazing designs and – most importantly – the final product has high enough resolution and looks great on any online or print platform.

4. **Add white space.** Sometimes when we have a lot of good information to share, we try to cram it all onto one graphic. There are some infographics that have a lot of information and they look amazing – but there are more that simply contain too much. Leave some white space so people aren't overwhelmed. And if you start to feel like you have too much information on your graphic, ask yourself if you should be creating multiple images instead of trying to get everything into one space.

5. **Learn how to use software or a tool for creating infographics.** Many programs are highly intuitive – which can end up working against the users by lulling them into a false level of confidence that they are maximizing the benefits of the tool. Once you choose the tool you'd like to use, take the time to complete a few training videos. The tricks you learn will help you be more efficient, so it will be time well spent. Plus, you'll probably be inspired by some of the ideas they share!

6. **Keep it short (and narrow).** Similar to the idea of leaving white space, it's important to be discerning about what information you share. But for a graphic, keeping it short has one additional meaning as well. Consider the platform you'll be using the graphic on and make sure the image isn't too long or wide to be viewed easily.

7. **Brand your material.** If you create an amazing image, people will share it! It's an excellent way to drive traffic to your sites. Make sure your brand is prominently

displayed on your creation so everyone knows the original source.

8. **Inform without selling.** A graphic can be a great way to help someone solve a problem. If you have steps, a decision-tree, or any kind of image that supports a challenging process a person is working through, offer the solution without any strings attached. Be the person everyone wants to know and – as long as you remember to use branded material – people will associate those positive attributes with your products.

9. **Add description and tags.** If no one can find your graphic, it doesn't matter how good it is. Remember to add a description and tags to the extent possible based on the platform you're using.

10. **Answer a question.** Similar to video, a graphic can be an amazing way to answer a question in your industry. And if people like your answer – if it's clear and concise, informative, etc. – not only will they appreciate the content, they will likely share it, helping you get your brand out to more people.

Professional Networking Sites

Watching the growth of professional networking sites around the world – Xing, Plaxo, Sumry, and, of course, LinkedIn – further supports what social media strategists have understood for years. Social media is the perfect space for professionals interested in making meaningful connections.

Top Ten Professional Network Tips

We've collected the most common themes from social media professionals, marketers, educators, and business professionals. These are best practices that will work in almost any industry – and the majority of them aren't even that hard to do.

1. **Create an informative company page.** I know this feels like an obvious recommendation, but it's one that a lot of people overlook. Is your LinkedIn company page the same material from your website? Or have you taken the time to tailor information for LinkedIn to make it appealing to visitors?

2. **Create and manage a group.** One way to establish yourself as an expert is to start and manage a group on LinkedIn that relates to your product or brand. For example, if you own a coffee shop, you might start a group that talks about running successful cafes or working with international vendors. As long as it some-how enhances your professional credibility, it's a great addition to your LinkedIn account.

3. **Choose a group (or two) and be active.** Remember to listen to your community – don't assume that you're always the person who knows the most about a situation and should therefore lead the conversation. Look for active conversations that you can join and then become a meaningful contributor. Being an effective community member is a way of leading that a lot of people overlook.

4. **Create Showcase Pages.** LinkedIn describes Showcase Pages as:

   i. *"A Showcase Page allows you to extend your Company Page presence by creating a dedicated child page for [particular] aspects of your business. Interested members can then follow your Showcase Page as they follow any Company Page.*

   ii. *"Showcase Pages are designed for building long-term relationships with members who want to follow specific aspects of your business, and not for short-term marketing campaigns. It makes sense to create a Showcase Page when you want to establish a dedicated page to represent a brand, business unit, or company initiative. Before creating a Show-case Page, ensure that you have a plan for maintaining an active presence."*

iii. Showcase Pages are a way to shine a light on some of your offerings and make it easier for people to find your products.

Deluxe Corporation

Financial Services
5001-10,000 employees

Financial Services at Deluxe

196 followers
+ Follow

Bags & Bows Online

137 followers
+ Follow

1. **Blog.** LinkedIn recognized that many users were sharing links to their blogs through their profiles and updates. Why not allow professionals to share their insights directly on the platform? LinkedIn created an opportunity for people to easily create blog posts right in the LinkedIn platform – and they've gotten mixed reviews. Some people feel it's just another way to contribute to the excessive amounts of content online and that it isn't regulated enough. But others have managed to parlay their blogs into exposure for their brand as well as a way to enhance their professional credibility. Individuals who have integrated the tool into their strategic plan – thoughtfully contributing blog posts that support their organization's brand – have seen positive results.

2. **Use images.** We often think professional sites aren't the place for pretty pictures – business is all about words! Your professional profile is going out to *people* and people respond to images. You don't want to share memes or inappropriate content, but don't downplay the value of an informative graphic or beautiful image on your blog post.

3. **Creatively engage in your community – and talk about it.** In addition to joining a group, you also have the opportunity to engage – as a brand, brand representative or individual – and make a name for yourself within your community by participating in interviews, writing blogs, and connecting with other media sources. Once you've made your connection, share the final product (video, post, etc.) with your professional network.

4. **Ask for recommendations.** Generating more conversations around the amazing work your brand is associated with is key to gaining traction on professional networking sites. You likely have raving fans who just haven't thought to recommend you! Ask for a recommendation – you'll be surprised at the positive responses you receive.

5. **Post a video.** Like graphics, videos on professional net-working sites are often underused. If you have a professional video that demonstrates your skills or showcases your products, your personal profile or company page are the perfect places to share it.

6. **Be consistent.** Post updates. Share articles. Comment on posts. Schedule time every day - even if it's just a few minutes – to contribute to online conversations. People will be more likely to remember you if you contribute a little bit every day than if you contribute big chunks of information infrequently.

What should I post about?

One of the most common fears I hear from business owners, marketers, and even social media strategists is, "What if I post too much about my product – and then everyone blocks me?" Asking that question is good. It demonstrates that you are a considerate and ethical business practitioner. And it is a legitimate consideration, though you're probably more worried than you need to be.

Every social media platform moves quickly and contains a lot of content. The specific statistics vary by platform and by user, but consider some of these numbers from Statistic Brain and then ask yourself how likely you are to overwhelm your audience.

- There are 52,000,000 photos uploaded to Instagram every day.
- The average Facebook user has 130 friends.
- 9,100 tweets happen every second.
- The average person's attention span is 8.25 seconds.

It's important to be respectful of your audience and your community, but in the fast-paced world of social media, you aren't as likely to irritate people as you probably think. Other than the speed of social media and content others post that breaks up your messages, it's also important to remember that you're not posting the same message over and over again. You're speaking on behalf of your brand about the things your audience finds important, not just about your product.

Content Brainstorming Exercise

Imagine you've written a cookbook and you'd like to brainstorm content ideas for your social media plan. You might initially think of links to where people can buy your cookbook, featured recipes, or images from the cookbook with a link to the order page. But after a while, you'd realize simply telling people over and over again that your product exists doesn't make you a very interesting person to know. What else could you share?

Question	Answer	Content Ideas
What's unique about my product?	It's a collection of recipes perfect for people who don't have a lot of time but want to prepare healthy meals.	• Calorie information and prep times with specific recipe titles and pictures • Tag healthy eating or weight loss groups
Who is my competitor? What are they talking about?	I found five similar cookbooks. In reviewing their posts, I found that they talked a lot about time-saving tricks and getting your family involved in food preparation.	• Quality family time associated with preparing food • Stories about my own experiences with my family • Tag food/family bloggers
What's happening right now in my community that people are talking about?	How to spend after school/before dinner time is a hot topic as is how to get kids to eat vegetables.	• Share the video created by the local community center about family time • Share funny, kid-friendly games like "vegetable math" (counting, addition and subtraction)

If you get your team – or even peers who understand your business – together for a few hours and have everyone share every idea that comes to their mind, you will have more content to share than you can handle! And then you really won't have to worry about boring your audience because you'll mention your book, but you'll really be talking about things that interest your community. Here's how the cookbook example might start to shape up:

1. Cookbook sale – automatic 10% for anyone who buys a copy on Monday <link to purchasing site>
2. Recipe – share your TWO favorite ingredients on Tuesday <link to book>
3. Article in the local paper about a fair that featured your book
4. Video about quality family time
5. Vegetable math game description

You can easily contribute large amounts of content to conversations your audiences would be interested in. Without *selling* to them, you have the opportunity to continually get your product information in front of them and you establish yourself as a good person to know.

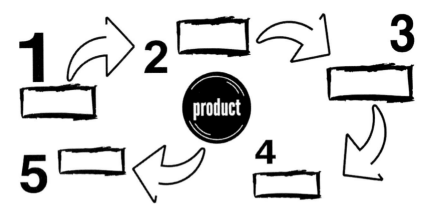

Still need more content ideas?

Expand your content idea chart by answering any of the following questions that might relate to your business. And remember: this works best with a group and every idea should be welcome. (Sometimes it's the wildest ideas that lead to the best content!)

- How was the product created? What short, funny stories could be shared?
- Which celebrities have a connection to your industry, brand or community? Are any of them in the news right now?
- What's happening locally related to your product?
- Who could you interview, who has had a positive experience with your product?
- What creative things have people done with your product?
- What charitable organizations are affiliated with your product?

Making Predictions

When Buffer published its State of Social Media 2016 Report, it provided social media strategists with the perfect information to make a wide range of educated decisions about their platforms. In the key takeaways section, they highlighted three important points – and each point represents one strategic approach marketing professionals can take when planning for the future.

According to their research:

1. Video is about to hit the peak! Now's the time to get on.
2. No one has left Facebook! Almost every marketer is using Facebook (93%) and Facebook ads (91%).
3. Only 1 in 5 respondents use social media for customer support.

Strategy #1: Recognize trends that still have life left in them – and join the crowd.

It was hard to miss the popularity of video in 2016. Facebook Live – though launched the year before – gained popularity and video on YouTube, Instagram, and Snapchat became the perfect mechanism for storytelling. Research tells us video is about to peak and we don't have any reason to doubt it. Don't look at statistics like the increase in video usage over the past year and worry that you missed an opportunity. Recognize that a trend has been identified and now is the time to act.

Strategy #2: Don't believe everything you hear.

2016 could be the year of video – or it could be called the year of fake news. We have seen an unprecedented amount of information misrepresented or simply falsified. By the end of 2016, it had become such an issue, Facebook and Google shared their plans to curb the circulation of fake news. But fake information isn't new to social media strategists; we've been managing it for years. We're constantly hearing what times we should post to guarantee success, which brand new trend is guaranteed to take off, and even which industry giants should be abandoned to make room for the next big thing. If this information comes from a credible source, give it some thought. It's certainly possible it has some merit and even if it isn't entirely true, there might be bits you can learn from. But when someone reports something like, "No one is on Facebook anymore – rewrite your entire marketing strategy," we encourage you to check a few other sources before making any changes.

Strategy #3: If a good idea hasn't caught on yet, it's your opportunity to lead the way.

20% of organizations using social media for customer support – an undeniably good idea – is a startling number. Are you missing something? Has it not caught on because there is an intrinsic fatal flaw that 80% of businesses are aware of that you simply can't see? While that might be true in some cases, there's also a chance you're ahead of the game. As a social media professional, you should be reading every bit of information you can get your hands on, watching video, and talking to your peers about best practices. If you've done your research and found a good idea, don't be surprised you're an early adopter of a smart trend. Start to expect that of yourself!

Continue to speak on behalf of your brand about the things your audience finds important. You'll naturally find opportunities to talk about your product and, when you do, they will appreciate your suggestions because you have established yourself as someone who cares about making meaningful contributions to the community.

Chapter 6 Discussion

1. Commit to using one of the tips listed in this chapter for each of the social media platforms you are active on.

2. As a social media professional, you may be part of a team or solely responsible for your organization's social presence. Either way, discuss at least one of the tips in this chapter with someone in your organization. If possible, ask them to commit to trying the technique to support your social media strategy.

Part Four
Sharing

Chapter 7

What's Published Where?

Once you have created your high-quality content, you will need to determine what to publish on various platforms. Here are a few key considerations to get you started:

1. What platform(s) does your audience use?
2. What's the most common kind of engagement on those platforms?
3. What are realistic goals (based on the size of your community and typical activity on the platform)?
4. How much time do you have and how many platforms can you manage well?

If you completed your STP analysis and determined that your audience is on YouTube (question #1), you would note that consumers can watch videos (briefly, in their entirety, or any amount in between), like or dislike them, leave a comment, subscribe to the channel, or share the video (question #2). You might further investigate how your audience typically engages (likes, comments, etc.) by looking at your previous posts and what your competitors have posted.

While researching how your audience engages, note the average level of engagement (question #3) and what factors are common in the more popular content. Be sure to consider content, quality, and any tags or keywords.

Finally, it's time to reflect on your own resources. You've had the opportunity to consider what content is needed to be successful. Do you currently have the resources to keep those platforms active? If not, what can you do (reallocate resources, outsource work, etc.) to be successful?

The following is a list of ideas any business can apply to their marketing plan. Each will look different in different organizations and will involve varying levels of time and energy depending on the existing plan. Wherever you or your team are in the process, it's beneficial to review each consideration and identify how it might apply to your success.

Rinse and Repeat

In your marketing plan, you likely identified multiple platforms where your audience is active. For each platform, answer the same questions – how people engage, realistic goals for your business, and whether you have the resources to make that happen. In the previous section, you had the opportunity to dig in and think about what kinds of content you could share on social media – now is your chance to think about all the places that content can flourish and how people will enjoy it.

Consider the following examples as a starting point:

If you have a blog, in addition to sharing your post on all your sites, have you considered:

- Using quotes from posts to create infographics
- Reading the post and sharing it as an audio file
- Creating a video for YouTube with the highlights (including the link to the original blog in the description)

If you have a strong following on LinkedIn, have you thought about:

- Sharing images and infographics in your updates instead of just text
- Writing about a part of your journey – not just the finished product (e.g., "I'm recording my first audio book today and have been preparing all week – wish me luck!")

- Automatically tweeting your updates (even if they exceed the character limit of Twitter)

If you've created an amazing infographic, have you tried:

- Sending it directly (via a platform or email) to someone who might be interested in it
- Creating a video around the graphic – zooming in and out or highlighting various pieces
- Writing about the image – sharing the written description as a blog post

History is Your Greatest Predictor

If you have created your strategic plan, you should have carefully mapped out your core audience. This may evolve over time or suddenly if a significant event alters your product or brand's initial course. But what has worked well in the past – once you figure out why – will be your best indication of success in the future.

Review Past Activity

All of your past social media activity lands somewhere on the success spectrum. As a social media strategist, it's your responsibility to figure out why.

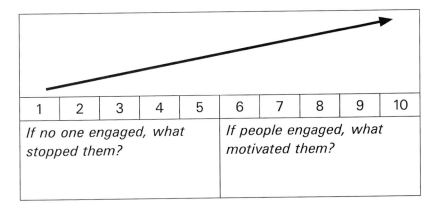

1	2	3	4	5	6	7	8	9	10

If no one engaged, what stopped them?   *If people engaged, what motivated them?*

If people engaged, what motivated them?

We do want you to enjoy your success. If fact, one key to success in any job is having fun at work! But don't get so caught up in celebrating that you miss the opportunity to analyze why you had the success you did. Did the time/date, topic, hashtag, event, tagged account, etc. make the difference? Was it some combination of factors? You have the best chance of accurately identifying the source of your success as soon after the successful activity as possible. If you begin your analysis while the post is still very active, you may even find ways to continue to capitalize on the activity.

If no one engaged, what stopped them?

Social media moves quickly. There's little value in dwelling on posts that didn't do well. However, there is value in reviewing an unsuccessful post – especially if you really thought it would take off – to see what might have gone wrong. If you initially thought the puppy in the team jersey would be a hit and it didn't get a single engagement, can you figure out why? Did you share it at the wrong time, miss an opportunity to provide a better caption – or is this not the right place for this content? You may find it was a fluke, but there's a greater chance it will give you valuable insight into your audience.

Focus on Your Customer

Scott Cook, co-founder of Intuit, was quoted as saying, "So I think instead of focusing on the competition, focus on the customer." Would you believe that we agree wholeheartedly? We recommend competitor analysis throughout all of the NISM books because there is much to be learned from the competition. But when it comes to social media engagement and what really works, your customers have your answers. Observing how they engage with you can tell you everything you need to know.

Don't Be Afraid to Try Something New

We talk a lot about what people have done successfully and learning from what's worked. That doesn't mean you shouldn't try new things! Don't be afraid to experiment with new approaches – surveys, live video, humor, an image without text. Changing your content might catch the attention of new customers or even re-engage your current audience. And if a new approach doesn't work, the experience will undoubtedly give you new insights to help you improve.

"In the spirit of science, there really is no such thing as a 'failed experiment.' Any test that yields valid data is a valid test."

- Adam Savage

Platforms

When you tell people that you work in social media, they might immediately ask you about an obscure platform or even a post that they're sure you've seen – because as a social media professional, you've seen everything that's on the internet, right? With immeasurable amounts of data being shared by the second, of course we can't keep up with everything. That's actually what makes *strategy* so important; it allows us to step back from the details and see trends that cross platforms and last over long periods of time.

The following is a list of ways social media professionals can share content. The techniques can be used on various platforms (e.g., you can blog on WordPress or LinkedIn) with minor modifications to accommodate for limitations or maximize opportunities on each platform.

Blogging

Whether you're publishing content to a company blog, a WordPress site, or LinkedIn, there are few tips that will increase your blog readership and engagement.

Before You Post...

- **Collect email addresses.** Even if you have an internal blog, send a push notification to let people know it's available.
- **Poll your audience or community for blog post ideas.**

In Your Post...

- **Craft a catchy headline.** Be clever, but be careful not to be too ambiguous or you won't engage the right readers.
- **Be consistent.** Post on a regular calendar when possible and choose a tone that is appealing to your audience.
- **Create "evergreen" content.** Unless it can't be avoided, create material that is timeless and can be easily shared in the future if the topic comes up again.
- **Be generous – don't provide incomplete information.** Once upon a time it used to be an effective technique to solve half of a problem and leave your audience wanting more – but with so many answers at our fingertips, that technique doesn't work anymore! Tell the whole story and establish yourself as a good person to know.
- **Be succinct.** As important as it is to tell the whole story, it's also important not to share any more than necessary. Respect people's time by organizing your thoughts and delivering your material efficiently.
- **Cite other sources.** Demonstrate that you've done your research and that this is more than just your opinion (unless it's an opinion post, of course).

- **Include a call to action.** You've impressed them with your post, now tell them what you'd like them to do! It can be as simple as engaging on social media and sharing the blog post or a more detailed task related to your content.

After You Post…

- Make your content sharable.
- Share on all of your social platforms.
- Respond to comments from your readers – on the blog post and your social platforms.
- Be patient; it will take time for your blog to gain popularity.
- Be consistent and keep your valuable posts coming.

Microblogging Platforms

Microblogging is the technique of sharing short pieces of information on platforms that typically move fairly quickly. The most common microblogging platform is Twitter (and we covered a list of specific tips for that platform in the previous section), but Google+ and Tumblr are also often included in this group. While many people only associate Twitter with microblogging, the term often refers to short, 200-word blog posts.

Wherever you are microblogging, consider the following tips to get the most out of each post.

- You have very limited space, so be sure to leave room for keywords.
- Use hashtags to start or join a conversation.
- Post consistently.
- Stick to content and themes that interest your audience.
- Set up alerts to help you find valuable content to share or respond to.

- Share credible content that's meaningful to your followers – don't post just to seem active.
- Just because your posts are short doesn't mean they can be thoughtless.

People have grown accustomed to finding answers quickly. As search engines become more and more effective, the art of microblogging is sure to increase in popularity and perceived value. Especially when users are looking for a quick answer to a question, this technique is an excellent way to connect with your customers.

Social and Professional Networking Platforms

Platforms like Facebook and LinkedIn allow users to focus on building relationships – personal and professional – as a brand and brand representative. For these scenarios, there are a few tips that are universally applicable for businesses.

- Follow the 80/20 rule: 80% of the content you share should be a gift to your customer. Only 20% (or less) is an ask.
- In addition to your logo (so people know it's really you), choose engaging and high-quality photos for your page and posts. Don't be afraid to be bold in your image selection!
- Fill out the "about" sections and additional information sections of your profiles. These sections are often overlooked and they are a great way for people to get to know more about your organization.
- Post a variety of content types. People often forget they can post video, infographics, and text. The variety in your posts is more appealing to your audience.
- Remember to talk about your brand (directly) and the things that interest your community in relation to your brand (indirectly).

- Monitor your page and respond to comments. If you ignore a response, you've done more harm than good!
- Consider boosting posts and promoting your page. Paid advertisements are incredibly effective and can be targeted for the exact audience you want to get to know.
- Don't be afraid to experiment with the number of posts, content, and time of day. But make your efforts count by tracking what's successful.
- Tag people and organizations as appropriate. Be thoughtful – don't tag people unless they'd genuinely benefit from the connection.

Whatever networking platform you're on, remember to be consistent with your brand. If one or multiple people are posting, it's important that everyone understands the voice of the organization.

Image-based Platforms

While photos are important on every platform, there are some platforms that hinge on great pictures. Instagram, Snapchat, Pinterest, and others put images first and text second. So how do you make your pictures worth a thousand words?

- Use high-quality images. There are sites like Pixabay and Morguefile that provide free images for commercial use, but it's also a great idea to invest in having professional photos taken of your product, office, staff, etc. Get organized and save some money – bring a photographer in for a day and get everything done at once.
- Take unusual pictures! Can you shoot from a unique angle? Is the sun creating the perfect bright spot? Are you able to snap a picture of a portion of something and leave the viewer wondering what they're looking at? In most cases, the more creative, the better.

- Test how the size and shape of your image works on the platform. Instagram is a square, while tall pins get more activity on Pinterest – so what do you do with your rectangular photo? When taking pictures and creating images, consider the shape your final format will be.
- Don't abandon text! Use descriptions and tags to help people find you and your images.
- Pay attention to which images are doing well with your core audience. Let them teach you.

Chapter 7 Discussion

1. Answer the four questions listed at the beginning of this chapter and summarize what options you will pursue for publishing content.

2. What's a new publishing technique you can try? What can you do to help ensure this new technique will be successful?

Chapter 8

Two-way Conversations

Two-way conversations typically refer to social media marketing professionals listening and responding to current and potential customers on social media. This concept is covered in detail in *Online Community Management: Grow and Develop an Active Audience on Social Media,* but it's important to cover the material here as well. A common and severe mistake some social media strategists make is focusing entirely on putting content out on their platforms, and they miss the opportunities that engaging with their customers provides. This, of course, leads to a disconnect from customer needs, as well as a general feeling that the organization doesn't care about its customers.

Before recapping some of the highlights associated with two-way conversations, we'd also like to mention the importance of reading, commenting on, and responding to the content or comments of your industry peers. While they aren't typically your customers, they're still potentially significant contributors to your success and shouldn't be ignored. Like your relationship with your customers, your peers can be a great source of industry information and inspiration. Reading and responding to their content is a great way to become a valued member of the community.

Why do we think two-way conversations are important?

In the first social media job study conducted by NISM in 2012, we asked survey participants about community management. In general, it was ranked as highly important. Comparing the 2012 and 2016 results, survey participants again ranked each of the five categories as very important. One of the notable results from the survey was directly related to two-way conversations.

- The perceived importance of two-way conversations with customers was given medium importance by the largest percentage of survey participants in 2012 (35.1%) whereas the largest group in 2016 (53.3%) ranked it as highly important.

If you have a community manager, they will likely take responsibility for keeping these conversations moving. Their goal is to constantly maintain the flow of information in multiple directions so people stay interested and engaged in the topic. Whatever the subject, the power of an online community is in the ability for many people to rally around a shared bond and feel empowered to contribute.

You have the opportunity to increase engagement through two-way conversations in the following ways:

- Launching simple opinion polls, then encouraging members to participate in the poll and comment on the topic being discussed
- Product and brand feedback (positive and negative)
- Concerns or suggestions related to the organization, industry or a current event

No matter what combination of these techniques works for your individual organization, one thing is true: you need active community members to make the conversations interesting. Once the conversations are going, your community will grow naturally. Active members will invite others, people will share content and you'll appear in more searches as you solve more and more problems and more people respond. The bigger your online community, the more opportunities you'll have to grow – often naturally and with very little effort.

Chapter 8 Discussion

1. What topics are most likely to generate conversations on your social media platforms? Brainstorm a list of ideas and share with your marketing team and/or leaders.

2. What metrics do you currently use to measure the frequency and effectiveness of two-way conversations? What metrics would you like to add?

Part Five
Paid Promotions

Chapter 9

Planning Your Ad Campaign

Within your budget and strategic plan, it's important to have some paid promotions – even if you start small. Businesses rely on paid promotions to varying degrees – often heavily influenced by budget – but a combination of growth through organic search results, community support, and platform ads is the strongest approach to reaching your marketing goals.

If you aren't convinced, check out some of these highlights from research conducted by Hootsuite in 2016:

- In 2016, total Promoted Tweet engagements were up 91% year-over-year—much higher than traditional banner ads.
- Ad recall from sponsored posts on Instagram was 2.9x higher than Nielsen's norms for online advertising.
- On Facebook, desktop ads have 8.1x higher click-through rates and mobile ads have 9.1x higher click-through rates than normal web ads.
- 100% of the top 100 global brands have run YouTube ads in the past year.

Reach has changed some over the last few years – primarily to the disadvantage of the business owner counting on organic reach to connect with new customers. But the good news is that paid promotions have become incredibly effective, so the money you invest – assuming you create an effective ad – is likely to yield very positive results.

In the first NISM textbook, a great description of social media advertising was presented.

"Traditional social media advertisement methods focused on messages in small spaces alongside newsfeeds and status updates designed to catch the attention of users. Paid social media advertising is designed to leverage social connections. Advertisements are usually tightly targeted. In most cases, you can reach specific niche audience groups with ads for your products and services, such as a certain age, gender, marital status, and so forth. In theory, this helps you put very targeted content in front of a customer who is ideally suited to consume it.

"Social media platforms also allow you promote your brand to get followers, likes, and so forth. The value of these 'purchased' likes is questioned by many social media experts due to the presence of fake accounts that like pages for pay, but don't actually interact with brands, and dilute the value of your audience. Social media platforms still have some work to do to win the full support of the online advertising community and prove the effectiveness of paid social media advertising as compared to other forms of online advertising, such as search engine advertising.

"If you are considering paid social media advertising, your ads should focus on raising brand awareness, and have clear, focused calls to action to capture the desired response."

How do you create an ad campaign?

The technical aspects of creating an ad campaign will vary by platform, but are often very similar, so a good place to start with any paid advertisement is to review current options, recommendations, and training through the platform.

As of 2017, the following social media platforms offer paid advertising and support for advertisers.

Platform	Advertising Support
Facebook	Facebook.com/business provides a well-organized list of articles and videos that can help you identify what ads you should run and how they should be set up. Additionally, there are resources available to guide you through the strategic process that will eventually help you choose your ad type.
Twitter	Social media professionals can find detailed information about Twitter ad campaigns at support.twitter.com or within the advertising site ads.twitter.com through the help menu. Like Facebook, Twitter has a variety of ad types, so you'll need to consider more than just your messaging.
Instagram	At business.instagram.com, strategists can find an overview of ad types (photo, video, and carousel) as well as an easy-to-follow list of how various advertising objectives can be met (reach, website clicks, video views, etc.). There are also detailed instructions for creating an ad.
LinkedIn	Since LinkedIn users tend to connect a little differently, it's a good idea to check out business.linkedin.com to review their unique offerings. They support the traditional sponsored content and text ads, but you can also choose sponsored InMail – which is an incredibly direct way to reach your audience.
Pinterest	You can learn more about promoted pins at business.pinterest.com by reviewing their ad standards and their creative guide. Pinterest has analytics and tactical considerations for you to review, but the site – and particularly the creative guide – are an excellent resource for creating pins that generate activity within the Pinterest community.
YouTube	YouTube.com/advertise walks potential advertisers through the key considerations associated with video advertising. They aren't too different from what you will uncover on other platforms – cost, targeting, measurement – but there is a piece about what video ads actually are that is beneficial for a user of any experience level to view.

A/B Testing

Once you know where you're going to advertise and understand the technical aspects of creating your ad, your next goal is to perfect the content. But with all of your options, how can you possibly know what works best? A simple process called A/B testing – modified as necessary by platform – can help you do just that.

A/B testing simply means running the same advertisement twice with a single change to the second post. For example, you might create two promoted tweets with the same text and a different image to see which picture garners a greater response. You could also run 2 Facebook promotions – one with an image and one with a video – keeping all other criteria the same as a way of gauging which media type your audience prefers and to what extent (e.g., did engagement increase by 2% or 200% with one ad).

Learn from the Success of Others

On each of these sites, you'll also find case studies that highlight how a business – undoubtedly like yours in some way – has used the advertising option successfully. If you view those stories simply as a source of inspiration, you're missing a great opportunity! Check out the details of what they did and why their campaigns were successful.

In addition to the case studies, there are others who have valuable content to share with you. Remember, you aren't alone in exploring social media advertising! There are a lot of people learning along with you and many have become experts through their research and application.

- **Expert videos.** A great way to learn how to post an effective ad is by watching someone else actually create one. Fortunately, the internet is full of videos created by professionals demonstrating their understanding of advertisements on specific platforms. A quick search is likely to bring up several good options that will walk you through best practices and the technical components you need to understand.

- **Hire help.** If it's in your budget, consider hiring an ad expert for the platform you're most interested in. You might hire them to coach you or to actually create an advertisement. Either way, working with someone who specializes in advertising on the platform you're interested in is a fast, hands-on approach to learning the ins and outs of potentially complicated platforms. At worst, you'll work more efficiently. At best, you'll gain insight into how to use the platform effectively.

Tracking Success

When you research your advertising options at each platform, be sure to pay close attention to the tracking options you have for each of your ads. Again, there will be a fair amount of variety between platforms, but consistently you will be able to track:

- Reach/Views
- Engagement
- Click-through

In addition to other measurements available on specific platforms that you have determined are important, the above data can help you determine just how effective your advertisement really is. Most importantly, while your ad is still running, it can help you make decisions about any adjustments that might make the remainder of your campaign more effective.

What about "native advertising"?

Native advertising matches the design of the platform upon which it appears. For example, a promoted Facebook post that appears in a user's feed (same design as other posts) would be considered native advertising.

If you've read *The Rules of Social Media Compliance & Governance: Know What You Need to Know*, your first thought was, "Doesn't the Federal Trade Commission (FTC) worry that this will equate to deceptive advertising?" If that was what you were thinking, you're right – the FTC *does* provide guidelines to ensure consumers understand native advertising is, in fact, promotion. They require visual cues, labels, and other techniques, like including the terms and tags "Advertisement", "Ad", "Promoted", "Sponsored", "Featured Partner", or "Suggested Post" in subtitles, corners, or the bottoms of ads.

General Guidelines

Whatever platform you choose, there are a few guiding principles that will always apply.

- Include a clear call to action that supports the goal of your ad.
- Consider carefully what content will be most beneficial. It isn't always "click here to buy." Sometimes thought leadership and information sharing can do more for your brand in the long run than one-time sales.
- Target friends of fans – there's a good chance that people who are connected share the same interests and those interests just might be related to your product.
- Use native advertising when you can to ensure people see your ad clearly on whatever device they are using.

As you explore paid advertising, remember to update your project manager regarding any changes or recommendations associated with the budget or strategic plan. Be sure, too, to share the impressive results of your paid campaigns with the team on a regular basis to ensure continued support from leadership.

Chapter 9 Discussion

1. What ad campaigns have worked well for you (in your current or previous role) in the past? Why were they successful?

2. Choose one platform whose campaigns you'd like to learn more about. What approach will you take (hire an expert, watch videos, etc.) to create an effective ad on the platform?

3. Choose one platform and answer the following questions:

   a. Who is your target market on this platform?

   b. Using A/B testing, what approaches will you try and why?

Part Six
The After-Party

Chapter 10

Review Your Strategic Plan

It can be so exciting to craft all kinds of creative social media content! In fact, it can be so exciting that you might forget about the traditional marketing your organization is already using or should consider because of its past success. If you have created a solid strategic plan and your project manager is on point, you'll probably get a reminder to integrate the two marketing approaches. But where do you start?

Traditional and Social Media Marketing: Together Forever

There are some companies that forgo either traditional or social media marketing techniques, but the majority will find a way to use them both – and to make them work together. The following is a list that outlines key considerations that can help you make sure your traditional and social strategies are not only aligned, but supporting each other.

1. **Verify that you use the same branding.** Your style guide should include the same guidance for traditional and social media. While not everything will apply to both, wherever there is overlap, the branding must be the same.

2. **Promote your social media platforms in your traditional marketing materials (and vice versa).** Add your social sites on flyers. Promote your printed catalog on your social sites. Look for opportunities to cross-promote as often as you can.

3. **Pull stories from one format to the other.** Read quotes from your social sites in your radio commercial. Post clips from a TV spot featuring your product on your Facebook page. Oftentimes a great opportunity will start on one type of marketing but transition beautifully to the other.

4. **Get your sales staff on social media.** If you have a strong individualized selling approach, encourage those people to contribute to your digital presence as well. They are so close to the product, they will have amazing insights to contribute.

5. **Use social media as the organizing component of a traditional marketing approach.** For example, if you had a product launch at a local mall, you could have people enter to win a drawing at the mall by using a hashtag on Twitter.

6. **Look for opportunities to use communications created for one approach in the other area.** Did your top salesperson just deliver an amazing presentation? Put it on SlideShare. Transcribe it and post it to the company blog. Create short video clips featuring the highlights.

The theme that clearly emerges when you examine the process of traditional and social media working together is more than consistency in branding – which is undeniably important! It's also about making the most of the incredibly valuable connections marketers make with both approaches by communicating tactics within the organization's strategic plan.

Chapter 10 Discussion

1. Review your strategic plan with one goal in mind – identifying opportunities for traditional and social media marketing to complement each other. After you review

each piece of active traditional and social media marketing, also note what could be added to the mix.

2. What is the best way to share what you learned with the rest of your organization? Create a document or presentation that outlines the opportunities you uncovered as well as the areas where the organization is already succeeding.

Chapter 11

Key Stakeholders

What do your company stakeholders know about your core audience?

We spend a lot of time talking about talking to customers, but how often do we make time to gather information from key stakeholders in our organization? It's often assumed that because of their status, their voice will be heard no matter what, so there's no reason to actively integrate them into the conversation. But what can we learn from them, when should they be approached – and how should we ask?

What

Share specific questions instead of simply asking, "What do you think of this idea?" People – key stakeholders included – will have an easier time sharing valuable feedback in response to a specific inquiry. "We chose this approach and budget based on this research. Would you make any changes?" is more likely to garner a valuable response than, "Please review our plan and let us know what you think."

When

As soon as you have enough details to share, connect with your key stakeholders. If you wait too long, using their valuable feedback may become difficult or costly. Sharing too early has a downside, too – you don't want to have to circle back with changes. But as soon as you have a concrete idea, seek feedback.

How

One of the most frustrating complaints I hear from social media strategists is that they asked for feedback and didn't get it – or got it too late. At the root of that problem is usually how the feedback was requested. For some people, a short meeting where the idea is described to the key stakeholder works well. (Feedback is immediate.) For others, a concise written description allows the stakeholder to review it on their own time. (In those cases, use highlights and bullets for the main points to make reading faster and easier.) Remember: It's unlikely your key stakeholders have an intimate knowledge of social media. If you provide too much information or if the delivery is convoluted, they won't be impressed by the quantity of information you've shared. They are more likely to be irritated at your inability to be succinct – and that's if they read it at all. Like your social media content, keep your message clear and concise.

Take the time to invest in understanding your core audience and key stakeholders. Your time will pay off in more ways than you expect – including boosting your reputation as a social media professional.

Updating Key Stakeholders

Keeping key stakeholders informed is critical for any social media professional, but updating them regarding marketing and communications can sometimes be tricky. When we completed our most recent job study, we had the opportunity to ask consultants, employees, and leaders about keeping key stakeholders in the loop. We wanted to know:

- How do your leaders and key stakeholders support your efforts?

- How do you keep key stakeholders aligned?

"Not only are we managing the brand presence, but we have a whole strategy mapped out for our CEO and our COO. We have five presidents, and they're all tweeting and on LinkedIn and doing thought leadership and have a whole different objective than the brand objective, but they complement each other."

"We got all the key functional leaders in a room, and no one could leave until we had a plan in place. And then we had a review panel for communications, with different people on point for different things. But it's interesting because in those situations, the communication lead ends up leading the group not so much on the solution for the problem, but on all the actions that are going to take place until the problem is solved because they're so directly related to what we have to be able to communicate, and we wanted to be able to communicate that we were doing things. So it ended up that we met twice daily, we did two daily client communications, and coordinating with all the different teams to make sure that they understood what we were saying where; if they got a call, what to say; and how to do FAQs and all that kind of stuff. So it ended up being a pretty big plan, but it worked well, so it was worth it. And at the time, it was the most important thing to do for our business, so we had all hands on deck."

The themes were clear. Planning and communication were critical to getting key stakeholder buy-in and keeping them engaged. Social media professionals often meet resistance from stakeholders who feel too busy to review status updates or question results that aren't tangible. As social media professionals, we have to push through the resistance and commit to sharing updates. If we don't, we risk stakeholders becoming removed and possibly doubtful of the value of our work.

Chapter 11 Discussion

1. Identify the key stakeholders in your organization. Create a chart with three columns and list their names, their areas of expertise and the best way to communicate with them. Share this information with your team or just keep it as a reminder for yourself when you request feedback.

Name	Expertise	Preferred Communication

2. What challenges can you anticipate when connecting with key stakeholders in your organization? For each challenge, list potential ways you can overcome the obstacle you've identified.

Part Seven
The SMS Exam

Chapter 12

What Do You Need to Know for the SMS Exam?

If you're reading this book, there's a chance you're preparing to take the certified SMS exam. This section presents the key topics you can expect to encounter during the exam, but even if you aren't taking the exam the following section is a good review of some of the highlights of what's covered in this book. Review the following list and refer back to the text or to external resources as needed to ensure you thoroughly understand each topic.

Who is in your core audience?

Make sure your marketing efforts aren't wasted. Identify your core audience and target your marketing accordingly. You might feel confident that you know who your core audience is, but it's a good idea to go through segment, target and positioning (STP) exercises as well as creating marketing maps to confirm your plan and possibly identify new opportunities.

How can you get your key stakeholders to identify who company customers are?

Our key stakeholders are often busy, hard-to-reach people, but there is a good chance they have tremendous insights into our market. Remember to keep things simple and focus on the what, when, and how of your plan.

It can also be beneficial to consider any unique contributions stakeholders might have. For example, someone who had previously worked very close to the customer would have valuable insights that would vary from the equally valuable insights of a stakeholder with a strong finance background. You may choose to ask or at least emphasize different questions based on their experience.

Take the time to invest in understanding your core audience and key stakeholders. Your time will pay off in more ways than you expect – including boosting your reputation as a social media professional.

Create a communications plan.

Social media professionals should carefully consider the unique challenges and opportunities of their situation, but the guide provided in this book can be applied to any organization. Essentially, the plan can be broken into two parts – the overarching information everyone needs to know and the platform-specific details.

If it's easier to remember the important components of a communications plan by looking at an example, refer back to the sample in this book. And – especially if you don't already have a communications plan – a great way to remember the process is to actually use it. Consider creating a communications plan from scratch.

Review how to publish content to company blog(s), microblogging platforms (e.g., Twitter), and social networking platforms (e.g., Facebook).

Review the lists provided throughout this book that outline how social media professionals can share content. The techniques can be used on various platforms (e.g., you can blog on WordPress or LinkedIn) with minor modifications to accommodate for limitations or maximize opportunities on each platform, so don't focus on specific platforms. Rather, consider the strategic approaches and techniques.

Contribute great content.

- Offer social media content that your customers perceive as valuable as opposed to selling.
- Create innovative ideas that connect with and provide value to your audience.
- Identify what social media content your customers perceive as valuable and how they prefer to interact with the company.
- Provide content that informs, entertains, and helps.
- Ensure all written and video social media content is brief, concise, and accurate.
- Read, comment, and respond to the content or comments of your industry peers.
- Ensure branding consistency across all social media platforms.

Use traditional media in conjunction with social media.

Organizations should always be looking for ways to make their traditional and social media marketing work together. The following is the list (with fewer details) provided in this book outlining key considerations that can help you make sure your traditional and social strategies are not only aligned, but supporting each other.

1. Verify that you use the same branding.
2. Promote your social media platforms in your traditional marketing materials (and vice versa).
3. Pull stories from one format to the other.
4. Get your sales staff on social media.
5. Use social media as the organizing component of a traditional marketing approach.

6. Look for opportunities to use communications created for one approach in the others.

Report status on a regular basis to management and key stakeholders.

Planning and communication were critical to getting key stakeholder buy-in and keeping them engaged. Social media professionals often meet resistance from stakeholders who feel too busy to review status updates or question results that aren't tangible. As social media professionals, we have to push through the resistance and commit to sharing updates. If we don't, we risk stakeholders becoming removed and possibly doubtful of the value of our work.

Additional Resources

Sample Creative Marketing Approach

The following is an example of a unique way of using platforms to engage with audience members. Innovative marketing ideas that provide value to your audience can come in many forms – including pure enjoyment. The following is an overview of how ABC's hit show *Castle* brought their main character to life – quite literally!

Richard Castle: Breaking the Fourth Wall

ABC's *Castle* was a police procedural comedy-drama starring Nathan Fillion as the protagonist Richard Castle. He was introduced as a successful crime writer looking for inspiration from the NYPD. Much to her disappointment, he was teamed up with Kate Beckett (played by actress Stana Katic), a detective of the NYPD.

Throughout the series, many attempts were made to make the show seem as real as possible, from in-character appearances of other authors such as James Patterson (allegedly a peer of Richard Castle) to references to current events. But the producers of *Castle* took their creativity one step further – they broke the fourth wall and created a life for Richard Castle in the real world. He published a series of books – all of which were mentioned throughout the television show – that viewers can still purchase. He has an author page on Amazon that includes his picture (Nathan Fillion the actor as Richard Castle) and a biography that describes his character's life on the show.

The real author went to great lengths to maintain the pretense that Castle is the author, including dedicating his books to characters in the television series and having Fillion's picture in the book's jacket as author. However, perhaps most convincing was having Nathan Fillion show up to book signings and publicity events in character as the author Castle. Fillion continued to act as Richard Castle throughout appearances and provided an opportunity for the public to engage with the brand directly. In addition, it provided an important cross-media marketing tool bridging the two stories.

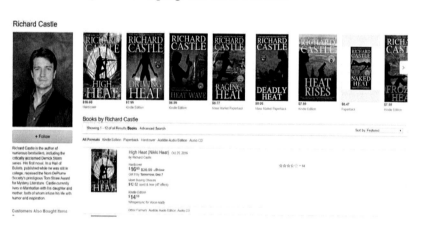

Castle's online persona was also convincingly realistic on social media. He was present in character on both Twitter and Facebook. The Facebook account was far less active than the Twitter account yet still garnered more than 4 million likes. Importantly, Facebook provided the opportunity for permanent images to help build his character's profile. Many of the pictures on his Facebook account involve relaxed and candid photographs of Castle with his on-screen family, undoubtedly posted with the intent of making the character's profile as believable as possible. However, with over 2,400 tweets to his credit and roughly 140,000 followers, Twitter is where the Castle character was most effective. The language and tone of his tweets kept with his on-screen persona.

Richard Castle @WriteRCastle · Feb 29
A Birthday toast to all those Leaplings out there. (Might be a few decades before your 21st birthday, but we'll celebrate anyway.)

 4   73   ♥ 278   •••

Richard Castle @WriteRCastle · Feb 24
I normally love starting the day off with the crossword, but after Monday, I'm a little puzzled out.

 10   120   ♥ 417   •••

Richard Castle @WriteRCastle · Feb 16
Anybody know a chiropractor? I've had my ribs crushed one time too many by a big Russian, and Alexis is getting tired of cracking my back.

 25   86   ♥ 361   •••

Richard Castle @WriteRCastle · Feb 15
DISCOUNT CHOCOLATES AT DUANE READE TODAY!!!!!!!!!

6   56   ♥ 219   •••

In the series, Castle was roguish, charismatic, and had a unique dry sense of humor, all of which carry over well to social media and make for entertaining and retweetable comments. However, to really give his online character depth, his tweets often cited current events. For instance, he tweeted his condolences after the Boston Marathon bombings in 2013 in character, and while it may seem insincere coming from a fictional character it was one of his most liked and retweeted comments. Furthermore, he referenced activities in his off-screen life, mentioning going on holiday when the show is off-season over the summer or playing board games at night with his fictional daughter Alexis.

Where he was most impactful is in making references to important events from the show. One such example is when his love interest Beckett shows up at his door unexpectedly during a storm for the season 4 finale. Deftly, the creators seized the opportunity to integrate the scene and promote Castle's new novel *Unholy Storm* with a play on words in one single tweet in May of 2014,

> "#UnholyStorm was unleashed yesterday. I remember an unholy rain storm a couple years ago that brought someone very special to my door."

Tweets like these resonated with the audience and are again some of his most retweeted and liked comments. This tweet perfectly sums up what a successful twitter account can accomplish. It seamlessly drew together both the new book release and one of the most pivotal moments in the plot from the show, creating an immersive experience for Castle's followers.

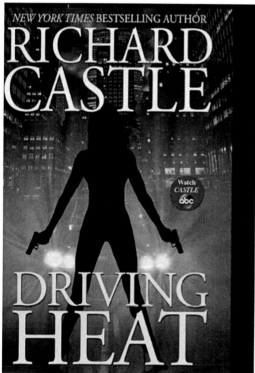

The show's Facebook page further blurred the line between fiction and reality by promoting Castle's books, and the fans enjoyed it. When the show was on the air – and even, as you can see in the above example, after the show had been cancelled – fans enjoyed talking about the books, the characters, and their great ideas for the show.

Why would *Castle* keep these conversations going after the show ended? This is an excellent example of the difference between providing your audience with random content and following a specific strategy.

1. *Castle* may have ended, but it was a popular show on a large television network – a network that will launch other similar shows that might appeal to the *Castle* audience. If you ever have a product that is phased out – especially if it's associated with a larger brand – leave your audience as happy as possible.

2. Products – the books, episode downloads, merchandise, etc. – are still available for sale and while they're certainly not a primary profit source, they are part of the brand that can live on past the show's original run time.

3. An active community clearly formed as a result of the successful show. That audience is a great fit for other shows – shows that are more likely to be successful if they start with an existing fan base. As a crime drama, the network's new show *Conviction* is similar enough to *Castle* to share an audience. The larger ABC brand can greatly benefit from keeping the audience content.

Glossary of Terms

Audience
Anyone receiving the information an organization is sharing.

Blog
A usually informal or conversational compilation of short articles, typically related to one subject.

Blog Post
A single contribution to a blog.

Brand Sentiment
The opinion or emotion associated with a brand.

Communications Plan
An outline that provides individuals and groups with the direction needed to share and respond to content on public platforms when representing a business or organization.

Community
People who are regularly engaged with your digital presence.

Core Audience
The people who the organization wants to receive the information because they are most likely to engage.

Event Hashtag
A tool used to bring all of your conversations and event information together on one platform.

Fourth Wall
The imaginary wall the separates audience members from characters on screen. "Breaking the fourth wall" refers to when characters speak directly to the audience either through the camera or by appearing in the real world.

Hashtag
Word or phrase preceded by the pound sign (#) used to start or join a conversation around a specific topic.

Key Stakeholders
Individuals directly affected by the organization's actions and/or influential people able to contribute to or stop specific activities within a business.

Market Map
Grid that represents current or potential customers based on two criteria.

Microblogging
Short, frequent posts on a blogging or microblogging platform.

Real-time Monitoring
Tracking conversations surrounding your brand, current trends, and topics.

Segment
Group of prospective buyers with common needs and responses to a marketing technique.

Traditional Media
Advertising types other than social media that typically include television, print, and radio ads as well as direct mail.

Twitter Party
A live chat on Twitter using a hashtag and meant to connect with new people.